Pewter-Working
INSTRUCTIONS and PROJECTS

by

Burl N. Osburn

and

Gordon O. Wilber

Dover Publications, Inc.
New York

Published in Canada by General Publishing Company, Ltd., 30 Lesmill Road, Don Mills, Toronto, Ontario.
Published in the United Kingdom by Constable and Company, Ltd., 10 Orange Street, London WC2H 7EG.

This Dover edition, first published in 1979, is an unabridged republication of the work originally published by International Textbook Company, Scranton, Pa., in 1938 under the title *Pewter-Spun, Wrought, and Cast*. This edition contains a revised and updated list of suppliers.

International Standard Book Number: 0-486-23786-9
Library of Congress Catalog Card Number: 78-74121

Manufactured in the United States of America
Dover Publications, Inc.
180 Varick Street
New York, N.Y. 10014

Table of Contents

"You long for simple pewter."
—Don Alhambra, from Gilbert and Sullivan:
The Gondoliers.

Introduction

THE underlying plan of this book appears to be as simply and as logically developed as economy and tradition require. The work is much more, however, than an elementary presentation of basic processes such as forming, soldering, casting, planishing, raising, decorating, and spinning; because these are but means to the more significant contribution which the authors have achieved.

As new techniques are introduced, they are fully developed. As the book progresses, many of the simple details of construction begin to drop away simply because there is no need for repetition, and the many creative and cultural possibilities of pewter are revealed. These open up a whole vista of opportunities which should result in an unusually satisfactory outcome for both the amateur and accomplished craftsman *in any of the soft metals*. It seems to me that this feature provides an index to the real worth of this particular contribution.

The authors, besides having long been master craftsmen in pewter, are personally acquainted, through wide travel, with the principal museum and private collections of pewter, and have done much in connection with their respective teacher education programs to develop interest and craftsmanship in pewter in the United States. In this, they gratefully acknowledge the very real pioneering work and writings of Augustus F. Rose, Director of Industrial Arts in the Providence, Rhode Island, schools, and of William H. Varnum, Chairman, Department of Art Education, University of Wisconsin.

William E. Warner

Illustrations*

*Most of the articles illustrated throughout this textbook and not otherwise accredited, have been made by one or both of the authors, or by their students. Some of the working drawings provide complete dimensions, for the benefit of the beginner. Others offer a few over-all measurements, which may be used as suggestions by the more experienced designer.

Chapter One

The Story of Pewter

THE "STORY OF PEWTER" is a narrative of service to mankind. Pewter has played an important part in the development of civilization, both as a medium for artistic expression and as a material from which domestic utensils were fashioned. The bronze used by the ancients was composed of a large percentage of copper and a smaller amount of tin. Now the complement of this alloy, that is, a large proportion of tin with a small amount of copper, gives an excellent form of pewter. Whether the reversal of the proportions of these two metals came first as an accidental mismeasurement of

(Courtesy of the Johnson-Humerickhouse Memorial Museum, Coshocton, Ohio)

Fig. 1—Examples of Oriental Pewter

the two ores, or whether it was due to experimentation, whether aimless or purposeful, has not been determined. However, it is known that the use of pewter had its inception at a relatively early date, a fact evidenced by the pieces of Chinese and Japanese ware that have survived for many centuries.

The contributions of ancient Orientals to the pewter heritage must inevitably preface any attempt to trace its early history. It was used by these peoples at least two thousand years ago. And not only was it used, but great skill and craftsmanship had been developed in its manufacture. Remarkable ability and taste were shown in the many specimens of artistic workmanship in pewter which later craftsmen have failed to emulate. Fig. 1 illustrates the beauty of line and proportion which is characteristic of their work.

The fact that the alloy used by the Japanese and Chinese contained a considerable percentage of lead made it easy to work, but rendered it of little use for table or domestic use. Hence, much of their pewter ware is found in the temples where it is used for religious purposes, or in their homes, where it serves as decoration or for personal adornment. Extant pieces include many examples of unique and artistic candlesticks, incense burners, and other altar pieces.

(Courtesy of the Johnson-Humerickhouse Memorial Museum, Coshocton, Ohio)

Fig. 2—Decorated Oriental Pewter

Oriental workmen enhanced the attractiveness of their pieces by surface decoration. Engraving was the most usual method of decoration, but inlaying pewter with other metals was also practiced. Gold, copper, and brass were used, as well as such materials as jade and ivory. In Fig. 2 are shown three fine specimens of antique Oriental pewter, the engraving being plainly discernible on two of them.

The influence of Oriental pewter making upon later developments in Europe is problematic. Since no record of an interchange of ideas on this subject has been found, it seems likely that the two developments were parallel and independent.

The Romans knew and used pewter, but only a few pieces of their work have survived. These specimens, however, point to the common use of this metal at an early date. At the time of the Roman invasion of Britain (55 B.C.) considerable skill had been developed in the working of this material. Besides utensils, the Romans used pewter for coins and seals of office. Many of these relics have been found in England, where they were left during the Roman occupation. Most of the pewter of this period was characterized by a sturdy simplicity. Utensils were produced for use, not for appearance, and consequently little attempt seems to have been made at decoration. The Roman contribution to the pewter heritage consists mainly in extending its use to most of that area now included in western Europe.

The period of the Dark Ages veils the beginnings of pewter making in most European countries. However, with the dawn of the Renaissance most countries were well advanced in the arts of working this material. France showed a marked development.

While early writings and extant pieces seem to indicate that much of this pewter was used for purely domestic purposes, it is for the elaborately decorated "show pieces" that French pewter is most famous. French craftsmen found in pewter a medium through which to express their artistry and skill. Pieces which have been preserved command the admiration of those who admire workmanship of the highest order. The ornate fruit dishes of Fig. 3A are representative of 18th century French artistry, while the Mass cruets of Fig. 3B portray the advanced state of French or Flemish craftsmanship of the same period.

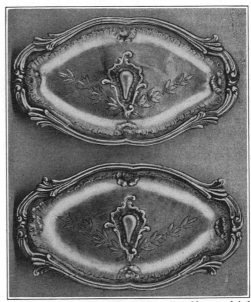

(Courtesy of the Metropolitan Museum of Art)

Fig. 3A—Pair of Fruit Dishes; French Pewter, 18th Century

Contemporaneously with the rise of pewter work in France and Flanders, a similar development took place in Germany. Just how early German work in pewter began is questionable, but the records seem to indicate a well-established industry as early as the eleventh century. There appears to have been two distinct types of pewter utensils produced by German craftsmen. For domestic and strictly utilitarian uses there were plates, bowls, spoons, salts, cruets, and similar articles. Much more interesting, however, are the highly decorated pieces now commonly found in museums and private collections. In this class are elaborately ornamental pieces closely resembling those of the French masters. The plate depicting the Imperial Electors, Fig. 4, is of historical value. Besides plates, these pieces included cups, beakers, and various types of flagons. Many craftsmen engaged in the production of pewter during the long period between the rise and decline of German pewter making. Features of their work are a superiority of design and an unusual achievement in artistic decoration. German pewter is represented by some of the rarest pieces now known.

Much fine pewter was made in other parts of Europe. Examples of work produced in Holland, Switzerland, and Hungary show the important place which this metal held in artistic and domestic enterprise.

Despite the widespread use of pewter in continental Europe, England was undoubtedly the p e w t e r center of the mediaeval world, to judge

(Courtesy of the Metropolitan Museum of Art)

Fig. 3B—Pair of Mass Cruets; French or Flemish Pewter, 18th Century

from the quantity produced and the number of pieces which have survived. The fact that the mines of Cornwall and Devon were the source of most of the tin used in olden times leads some writers to the supposition that pewter making started there. Be that as it may, the records show a well developed industry as early as Saxon and Norman times. Fragmentary records and occasional relics present a shadowy picture of early pewter making activities in England, but it is not until the thirteenth century that specific reference is made to the craft. At this time (1290) it was mentioned in the official documents that King Edward I had "leaden dishes" for cooking the boiled meats for the coronation feast.

Following this period the general adoption of pewter for cooking and eating utensils led to an increase in the number of workmen engaged in pewter making. Craftsmen early recognized the desirability of banding together for protecting their craft secrets, upholding the standards of production, and for social contacts. Indeed, in Germany there are indications that the workshops of pewterers in Augsburg were inspected by masters of the guild as early as 1324. Guild regulations placed restrictions on masters and apprentices, prescribed alloys, and set up examinations to deter-

(Courtesy of the Metropolitan Museum of Art)

Fig. 4—"The Electors"; German Pewter, Nuremberg, 17th Century

mine competency. In France, also, the guild early exerted a decided influence upon the pewter industry. Regulations for the Paris pewterers are of especial interest because of their similarity to those of the later English guild and their probable influence upon them. Most of the larger cities had their own guilds, and under their protection pewter making reached its highest degree of perfection.

Fig. 5—Typical English Touches

No account has been found specifying definitely when the pewter craftsmen of England first met together, but the first record of such a body was made in 1305. It was not until 1348, however, that the craft was officially recognized. Another 130 years elapsed before a charter was granted by the crown and the guild became known as the "Worshipful Company of Pewterers." This incorporation as a "Company" gave to the pewterers many powers which they had previously lacked. Such influence, increased by later grants, made it possible to set up and enforce rules and regulations, not only concerning the work of the pewterer, but also regulating the social and moral life of the craftsmen and apprentices as well. It controlled the most minute points of the pewterer's trade: the number of his apprentices and the length of their apprenticeship; the place where, and the time during which he was to work; the alloy he was to use; the method by which the vessel was to be cast, hammered, and turned; likewise, the marks and touches which he might use.

One of the most important functions of the Company was to keep a record of all persons engaged in the craft of pewter making. This end was attained by causing each member to have a mark or "touch." These marks were made with a steel die into which had been cut some ornamental or conventional design together with the name or initials of the maker. Fig. 5 illustrates some "Olde English touches." Many articles of pewter ware are stamped with various additional touches such as the "Rose and Crown" which indicated membership in the "Worshipful Company" or with marks of quality such as "Hard Metal" or with an "X."

A series of four small marks placed side by side and known as "Hall Marks" were also common. These marks were used on pewter as an imitation of those found on silver ware. A royal decree prohibited their use upon pewter, but only feeble attempts seem to have been made at its enforcement. Touch plates were kept in the Guild Hall, erected in 1485-1486, upon which every member was required to strike his touch or mark as approved by the Company. This regulation permitted a check upon the quality of all utensils produced.

(Courtesy of the Brooklyn City Museum)

Fig. 6—English Communion Set

The Company prospered and held an important place in the economic, political, and social life of England. Official records show that its influence extended over a period of five hundred years, during which time pewter ware was an important item in every household. It is undoubtedly due to the activities of the Company that English pewter maintained for so long a time its dominance over that of other countries, and that it is today regarded as exemplary of what is best in quality and workmanship.

The pewter ware of England produced during this period falls into two classes. There was that which was used for home and domestic purposes, including plates, saucers, tankards, mugs, and flagons. Measures of various sizes were common, the larger ones being used for flagons and the smaller for tankards. In addition to the pieces mentioned, table service demanded many small articles such as salt cellars, mustard pots, and pepper pots. Candlesticks were, of course, a household necessity, many excellent specimens of which have been preserved. Among the less common articles of pewter ware one occasionally finds tobacco boxes, chimney ornaments, inkstands, shaving basins, bleeding basins, caskets, belt plates, and maces. These articles and many others were in common use in the homes of England up to the period when china and porcelain appeared and usurped the place of pewter.

The second type of English pewter included all of that used for church or ecclesiastical purposes. It exhibits most of the sturdy, unadorned simplicity which one notes in domestic wares of that period. Typical pieces include chalices, patens, flagons, cruets, alms dishes, crosses, benitiers, and candlesticks, as illustrated by the communion set shown in Fig. 6.

Masters of the guild exercised extreme care in the inspection and control of the alloy used by its members, for frequent records relate to punishment meted out to offenders who dared to use other materials than those specified. Conflicting records leave much to be desired by way of accurate data on the exact content of early pewter. The best grade, known as "fine," seems to have been pure tin with as much brass or copper as it would absorb, which was about four to one. A less fine quality consisted of tin and lead, and the proportion here was also four to one. "Ley" or "Lay Metal" was the lowest standard and contained still more lead.

It was inevitable that many attempts should be made to improve upon the alloy used in making pewter. In 1652 a Major Purling invented an alloy which he called "silvorum" which looked very much like silver plate. However "the Pewterers' Company would have none of it," and as a result it was of little consequence. James Vickers of Sheffield was more fortunate. In 1769 he purchased from a workman who was ill a formula for making a white metal. The alloy is soft in texture, and looks so much like silver that the casual observer would be easily deceived. Examples of pieces made from this metal are highly prized by collectors, despite the fact that they are not real pewter. Another such development which had lasting results was the evolution of Britannia metal. This alloy seems to have been introduced at Sheffield during the second half of the eighteenth century as a means of competing with the rapid increase in the use of china and porcelain ware. It was produced by adding antimony to a high grade of pewter, thereby giving to the alloy whiter, harder, and more resonant properties. It seems to have been widely accepted, and its use largely displaced that of pewter. Thus is found growing up on the dying pewter industry a new development which continued its success long after real pewter had been supplanted.

Turning from the alloy itself to methods by which pewter articles were made, one finds that by far the greater part of the ware was cast. The molds, the most important item of the pewterer's equipment, were made from a form of bronze known as "gun metal." These molds were so expensive that they were frequently owned by the guild and rented out to individual members or groups. This circumstance accounts for much of the uniformity noted in the pewter ware of many localities. The story is told of one town in New England where all the spoons of the community had the same initial on the handle because of the constant use of the mold belonging to one family. Strangely enough, few of these molds seem to have survived the passage of years.

Large plates and chargers were difficult to make by casting and hence were hammered from flat sheets. The workmen engaged in making this type of ware were known as *sad-ware men*. They were the lowest paid and least respected of the pewter workers. Another branch of the craft known as *hollow-ware men* made large pots, measures, tankards, and flagons. A third group, known as *triflers*, specialized in making small pieces such as spoons, forks, buckles, toys, and buttons. The use of the lathe as a means of working pewter was limited to cleaning and polishing pieces which had been previously cast. Spinning of wares from flat sheets was prohibited by an ordinance of the "Company."

Besides that furnished to the homes of England, much pewter was exported to continental Europe and America. That which came to America, no doubt, served as examples for colonial craftsmen, and thus laid the groundwork for the American pewter industry.

There can be little doubt that during the early years of colonization, most domestic utensils used in America were products of English industry. Despite the fact that a few American craftsmen are known to have worked in pewter during the late seventeenth and early eighteenth centuries, it seems impossible that they could have supplied the demand for domestic articles which must have resulted from making new homes in a new land. Because of this domination of the American market by English wares, the style of American pewter was definitely set along English lines. Further, because the early American settlers, with few exceptions, came with a background of English craftsmanship, and English habits of thought and taste, they were accustomed to the type of utensils produced in England. Add to this the fact that the earliest pewterers of whom there is authentic record were Englishmen by birth or training, and the reason is evident why early American pewter followed the English tradition.

Despite the fact that much pewter was imported, the making of such ware in America must have started at a very early date. More or less reliable reports indicate that as soon after colonization as 1640 several pewterers were working in New England. Early centers of manufacture included Boston,

Newport, New York, and Philadelphia, but of the work produced before 1700, not a single piece has been found which can be positively identified.

The next period, extending from approximately 1700 to 1850, is undoubtedly the " Golden Age" of American pewter. During the first half of this time practically all of the dishes used were of pewter. During the latter half of the period new developments in china and porcelain assumed sufficient proportions to threaten the dominant place of metal utensils. It was during this century and a half that most of the really great American pewter craftsmen lived and worked.

(*Courtesy of the Johnson-Humerickhouse Memorial Museum, Coshocton, Ohio*)

Fig. 7—Early American Coffee Pot, by Sellows and Company

Their work included both flat and hollow ware. Plates, chargers, and basins stood in the oak or pine cupboard with beakers, tankards, and mugs. Spoons were cast and recast in great numbers. Other articles included lamps, candlesticks, ladles, skimmers, and strainers. In fact, it might be said that early craftsmen made from pewter most of those domestic articles now made in china, porcelain, earthenware, aluminum, tin plate, agate and enameled ware, and silver plate.

Most of the pewter made during this period was cast. Even the coffee pots so much admired today were made by this method. Two characteristic American coffee pots of the Pewter Era are shown in Figs. 7 and 8. Despite the freedom or lack of guild restriction in this country, little spinning seems to have been undertaken until quite late. Large plates, chargers, and platters were formed by hammering.

Not long after the beginning of the nineteenth century the introduction of

(*Courtesy of Alice T. Miner, Chazy, N. Y.*)

Fig. 8—Early American Coffee Pot, by Gleason

cheap porcelain plates removed from the pewter worker one of his chief sources of revenue. Deprived of this market he turned to the making of other articles for which there was still a demand. One of the most important of such

articles was the pewter coffee pot. So prolific were the pewterers in turning
out this particular utensil, and so universally did they engage in making them,
that this period (1825-1850) has been designated as the "Coffee Pot Era."
Entrance into this period was marked by a breakdown of old ideas of craftsmanship and the beginning of an era of mass production. With the end of the
first half of the nineteenth century even the making of coffee pots and lamps
(such as the specimen shown in Fig. 9) came to an end. Then that great and
important industry, which had developed and
nurtured so many American craftsmen, was
indeed a thing of the past. Making of pewter
had ended, but one still admires the many useful
and artistic articles which had been produced.

(*Courtesy of Alice T. Miner, Chazy, N. Y.*)

Fig. 9—American Chamber Lamp
with Saucer Base (height, 9¼
inches); made by Rust, New York,
about 1820

As some trees of the forest overtop the others,
so some American pewterers stand out from their
fellows as especially worthy. Judged by extant
pieces, one may mention such names as *Simon
Edgell*, to whom is attributed some of the oldest
known pieces of American pewter. He lived in
Philadelphia from about 1717 to 1742, was a
prominent merchant, and a friend of Franklin.
Especially famous are the two *Bassetts—John and
Frederick*—father and son, whose pieces are eagerly
sought by collectors. The German-born *John
Will*, who worked in New York from 1751 to 1762,
is held by many to be the leading American pewterer in matters of excellence of design and
quality of metal. *Henry Will*, the son of John, worked in New York and
Albany from 1760 to 1793. He has left a greater diversity of shapes than
any other eighteenth-century craftsman. *Cornelius Bradford*, of Philadelphia and New York, is famous for his plates, mugs, and tankards; as is also *William J. Ellsworth*, who worked in New York from 1770 to 1798. *William Will*, a
colonel in the Revolutionary War, was also a skillful pewterer. His pieces estab-
lish him as among the best of his time. He produced pewter ware in Philadelphia
from 1769 to 1798. Other outstanding names, many of equal distinction with
those already mentioned, include *Johanne C. Heyne* of Lancaster, 1754-
1780; *Thomas Danforth III*, of Rocky Hill, Connecticut, and Philadephia,
1778 to 1813; *Thomas D. and Sherman Boardman*, of Hartford, 1828-1854;
and *Samuel Pierce* of Greenfield, Massachusetts.

In addition to that of the *bona fide* pewterers, the work of that romantic
figure, "the traveling tinker," should be mentioned. Traveling from village to

village and farm to farm, on horseback or afoot, with his tools upon his back, he remelted, repaired, bought and sold pewter ware. One of his most common assignments was the recasting of spoons. This practice probably accounts for the scarcity of early spoons which bear the touch of known makers.

Ability to recognize and appreciate the pewter of early American craftsmen depends somewhat upon a knowledge of the "touch" mark which they placed upon their pieces. This system of marks grew out of and was patterned after the English system. In America, however, the lack of any strong organi-

Fig. 10—D. Melville

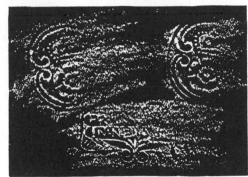

Fig. 11—Francis Bassett

Fig. 12—Frederick Bassett

Fig. 13—Joseph Danforth

Early American Touches

zation like the "Worshipful Company" gave more freedom for change and development in the matter of type. It also probably accounts for the fact that much early pewter was unmarked. For this reason it is sometimes suggested that an unmarked piece is more likely to be American than English or Continental.

Three rather definite changes occurred in American touches during the period up to 1825. The first 135 years (roughly from the era of colonization up to the beginning of the Revolution) were represented by marks which were closely akin to those used in England. The emblems include such features as the "Rose and Crown," the British "Lion" and the figure of "Britannia." These colonial imitations of English "touches" are illustrated in Figs. 11, 12, and 13.

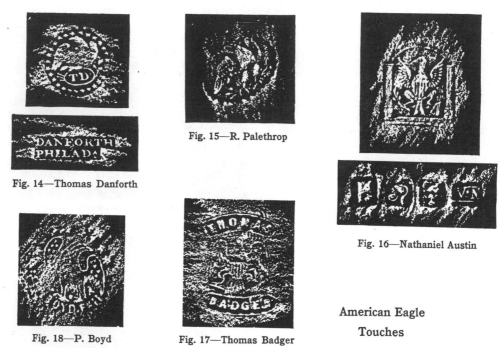

Fig. 14—Thomas Danforth

Fig. 15—R. Palethrop

Fig. 16—Nathaniel Austin

Fig. 18—P. Boyd

Fig. 17—Thomas Badger

American Eagle
Touches

A decided change in the character of the mark may be noted after the Revolution. Not caring to use touches showing a British character, the craftsmen either adopted some one of the state emblems (like that of Melville, Fig. 10) or developed a purely individualistic ornamental name plate. Then, with the close of the Revolution, individual pewterers hastened to put aside all of the old English symbolism and adopt that of the new nation. As a wave of patriotism swept the country, a group of eagle touches appeared and the symbol was immediately adopted by many. Out of twenty-three craftsmen who worked in pewter between 1790 and 1825, *at least* fourteen are known to have used eagle touches, some of which are displayed in Figs. 14, 15, 16, 17, and 18.

The making of pewter ceased to be a craft after this period and became a business. One is not surprised to see a change in the touches of the period.

The stately eagles soon died out, and in their places is found a simple mark with the name and address of the maker (Fig. 19). These trade-marks appear to have been stamped upon the pieces purely for business reasons, for with the passing of individual craftsmen there also vanished the pride of workmanship which inspired the artistic touches of earlier generations.

Fig. 19—A Touch of the
Coffee Pot Era

A study of pewter touches holds all of the thrill and glamor of real romance. By means of these simple marks early craftsmen who otherwise must have never been known have been made to live, labor, and create things of beauty and usefulness.

The manufacture of pewter, as such, seems to have been completely discontinued with the decline of the industry about 1850. Most of the companies retired from business while others went into new lines. Reed and Barton of Taunton, Massachusetts, and Homan and Company of Cincinnati, Ohio, were two concerns that survived by meeting the demand for plated ware.

Shortly after the beginning of the twentieth century, however, a revival of interest developed for things antique, and especially of the American colonial period. Several companies began the manufacture of antique reproductions in pewter, and others developed new designs. The use of pewter has increased since 1925 and today is preferred by many people to articles made from plated and other materials.

Fig. 20—Coffee Pot
Produced by Lester H. Vaughn,
Taunton, Massachusetts

Modern pewter ware, therefore falls into two types. For the person who prefers the antique, there are reproductions of early masterpieces. In some cases these are actually cast from original molds. For those who desire more modern styles, there is a wide variety of well-designed and well-constructed articles. Most modern manufacturers in adapting original designs, or producing new designs have kept the bold, simple lines which are the chief charm of pewter.

Fig. 21—Pitcher
Produced by Lester H. Vaughn,
Taunton, Massachusetts

Fig. 22—Porringers; Produced by Lester H. Vaughn,
Taunton, Massachusetts

Fig. 23—Reproduction of Tankard;
Produced by Laurits Christian
Eichner, Bloomfield, New Jersey

Fig. 24—Bowl and Ladle; Produced by Laurits Christian Eichner,
Bloomfield, New Jersey

Fig. 25—Coffee Set; Produced by Laurits Christian Eichner,
Bloomfield, New Jersey

Modern methods of manufacture differ considerably from those of the early workman. Much of the flat and hollow ware is now "spun" instead of cast. The stamping press is used frequently to produce unique shapes such as oval trays and gravy boats or to raise high forms in preparation for spinning. Casting is now restricted almost entirely to the making of such parts as spouts, feet, knobs, and ornaments. Machine methods for polishing have added many interesting possibilities in new and artistic finishes.

Among the contemporary American craftsmen who are working in pewter, some are confining their efforts to reproducing antique pieces, while others are attempting to use pewter in new and striking ways. Lester H. Vaughn of Taunton, Massachusetts, is well known for the excellence of design which characterizes his work, a distinction well deserved, as evidenced by the coffee pot of his production, Fig. 20, the pitcher, Fig. 21, and the porringers, Fig. 22. Laurits Christian Eichner of Bloomfield, New Jersey, is likewise notable among modern craftsmen. Three of his reproductions, the tankard, the bowl and ladle, and the coffee set are shown in Figs. 23, 24, and 25 respectively.

This revival and development in the making of pewter ware is also evident in many countries of Europe, notably the Netherlands, Sweden, and England.

Another result of the revival of interest in pewter has been its introduction into the schools. From small beginnings, this pursuit has rapidly spread over the country and now forms an important activity in many arts courses.

More recently still, it has been accepted by the home craftsman. The fact that pewter may be worked easily with small tools, spun on the average wood lathe, and melted and cast at a low temperature makes it an ideal medium for use in the home workshop.

Chapter Two

The Metal

MODERN PEWTER or Britannia metal is an alloy having a distinctive appearance and many desirable properties. It presents, when polished, a silvery white sheen and a soft tactual sensation unlike either silver or chromium plate, both of which it resembles to some extent. Old pewter, however, sometimes contains sufficient lead to cause the surface to assume a dark satin-like appearance with age, which many consider superior to that of modern alloys. Pewter weighs somewhat less than either silver or lead. A study of some commonly used thicknesses shows that fourteen-gauge pewter weighs approximately two and one-half pounds per square foot, while sixteen- and eighteen-gauge weigh approximately two pounds and one and one-half pounds respectively.

Pewter exceeds most other metals in ductility and ease of working. It may be stretched, compressed, and bent into almost any desired shape. Such processes are facilitated by the fact that it does not harden or stiffen appreciably under the tools, as is the case with copper, brass, and other metals. For this reason annealing is not necessary.

Pewter is somewhat softer than brass, bronze, and similar alloys. It may be cut easily with a pocket knife or with other edge tools. In spite of a softness which often results in articles being marred and dented, it must be classed as one of the most durable of metals. Given proper care, utensils made from this material will resist oxidation almost indefinitely. Pieces are still extant which were made two thousand years ago.

The melting point of pewter will vary with the composition, ranging from 425° to 440° F. An advantage of this relatively low melting point is the fact that it may readily be melted and cast.

Utensils made from Britannia metal have a high resistance to the action of almost all acids. Foods and drinks may be served in them without fear of chemical action.

Present-day pewter is an alloy composed of approximately 91 per cent tin, 7.5 per cent antimony, and 1.5 per cent copper. The best grades contain *no lead*. Tin forms the bulk of the alloy, which explains its soft sheen, ductility, and resistance to corrosion. The antimony serves to whiten the metal and to impart a hardness unknown to old pewter. The copper adds ductility and desirable working properties, but if present in more than a small percentage it tends to add an undesirable yellow color to the surface. Antimony gives an alloy the property of expansion when cooling. For this reason it is increased up to 15 per cent in some forms of casting metal. This addition tends to provide a sharp, clear impression in castings.

Pewter is available in a variety of forms, gauges, and sizes. The sheets are measured by the American (Brown and Sharp) gauge. It is commonly rolled in thicknesses from ten- to thirty-gauge and other thicknesses may be

(Courtesy of White Metal Rolling and Stamping Corporation)

Fig. 26—Casting Pewter Ingots

procured on special order. Pewter foil, which is about 36-gauge, is also available. The thickness most suitable for average work will range from 14- to 20-gauge with 16 and 18 the most popular. These sheets may be purchased in any size up to 24×36 inches. Sizes which seem especially useful for schools are 12×18 inches and 18×24 inches. It is also possible to obtain discs of pewter which have been cut accurately to size. Diameters from 2 to 16 inches and up are available, and it is frequently found more economical to buy pewter in this form. It should be noted, however, that some supply sources charge only for the weight of the discs, while others sell by weight of the square, and keep the scrap to cover cost of cutting.

Casting metal may also be purchased in the form of pigs and bars. The price is usually somewhat lower than for sheet stock.

A variety of findings is also available. These include pewter wire, both round and square, in sizes from $\frac{1}{8}$ to $\frac{5}{16}$ inch; rope wires from $\frac{1}{8}$ to $\frac{1}{4}$ inch; borders for reeding and decorating both plain, half round, and decorated. Tubing in a wide range of sizes, slugs for turning knobs, feet, stems, etc., and hinges of various sizes, may be purchased.

Technically the preparation of Britannia metal from its raw materials is a simple matter. However, experience and considerable skill are required to produce a metal which has the necessary characteristics of ductility and malleability needed for spinning, stamping, drawing, and casting. The copper is first melted in a crucible and enough tin added to produce a low melting mixture. The necessary amount of antimony is added, and finally the remainder of the tin. Great care is taken at all times to avoid over-heating of the tin; and to keep the mixture clean and free from dross and foreign substances. When thoroughly mixed, the alloy is poured into iron molds that produce slabs of metal which are usually about 1 in. $\times$ 6 in. $\times$ 10 in. The process is pictured in Fig. 26. After the removal of the pouring gate, these slabs are ready for rolling.

The rolls used in a typical rolling mill are made from chilled iron and measure approximately 12 inches in diameter. Starting with rolls but slightly closer than the thickness of the slabs to be rolled, they are gradually brought together until the desired gauge is obtained. Once a set of rolls is adjusted to a given gauge, as many sheets as desired may be run without further attention. The highly polished rolls produce sheets of smooth metal which require no further finishing. If the alloy thus produced is to be shipped, it is next taken to shears where the irregular edges are trimmed square and the sheets cut to standard sizes. If, on the other hand, the metal is for local consumption, it is taken directly to circle shears or a layout table and there cut into discs or blanks ready for use.

Numerous attempts have been made to find a suitable substitute for pewter which could be sold at a lower price. Alloys having approximately the same working characteristics as pewter are now available under such trade names as *Gar-Alloy*, *Eraydo*, etc. These zinc-base alloys have many characteristics which make them suitable for school work. They may be hammered, formed, soldered, spun, and cast in much the same manner as pewter. When finished they have a rather bluish-white color and a polish which may be preserved by coating with clear lacquer or shellac.

Chapter Three

Designing Pewter Ware

ONE MAY APPROACH the problem of designing pewter by analyzing the use to which the article is to be put and the surroundings in which it will be placed. If the furnishings with which it is to be associated are of some particular historic style, the pewter ware should be sympathetic with that background. This consideration requires a knowledge of historic styles in many fields.

If, on the other hand, the ware is to be used in a modern setting, the designer's first and foremost consideration is its optimum use. He must recognize that form follows function and so will be controlled by it.

The designer who seeks skill, should not only become familiar with the suggestions offered here, but should consult books dealing with the techniques and general principles of design. He should also form the practice of continually analyzing examples of work to learn why they are satisfactory, or in what ways they fall short of that goal.

The Historical Approach. It has been shown in Chapter 1 that pewter making reached a high degree of artistic craftsmanship during the many centuries of its use. In recent years there has been a wide interest in a revival of the study of historic styles of household furnishings of all kinds, with the result that many homes are furnished in antiques or good reproductions. If one wishes to design pewter ware for such a setting, it is necessary to consult reliable sources for accurate data.

One such source is the museum, where one may see and (by permission) examine fine pieces, or where photographs of the articles may be secured. There are also numerous private collectors of pewter who are willing to show their treasures to interested persons. If none of these aids is available, there are books which will be helpful to the designer who wishes to have his work historically correct. Several of these are listed in Appendix A.

With maturing judgment, the designer will learn many of the subtle characteristics of line and proportion that are often more influential in securing a spirit in keeping with the original than the most particular measurements could give. This judgment can come only from thoughtful, sympathetic experience, and study.

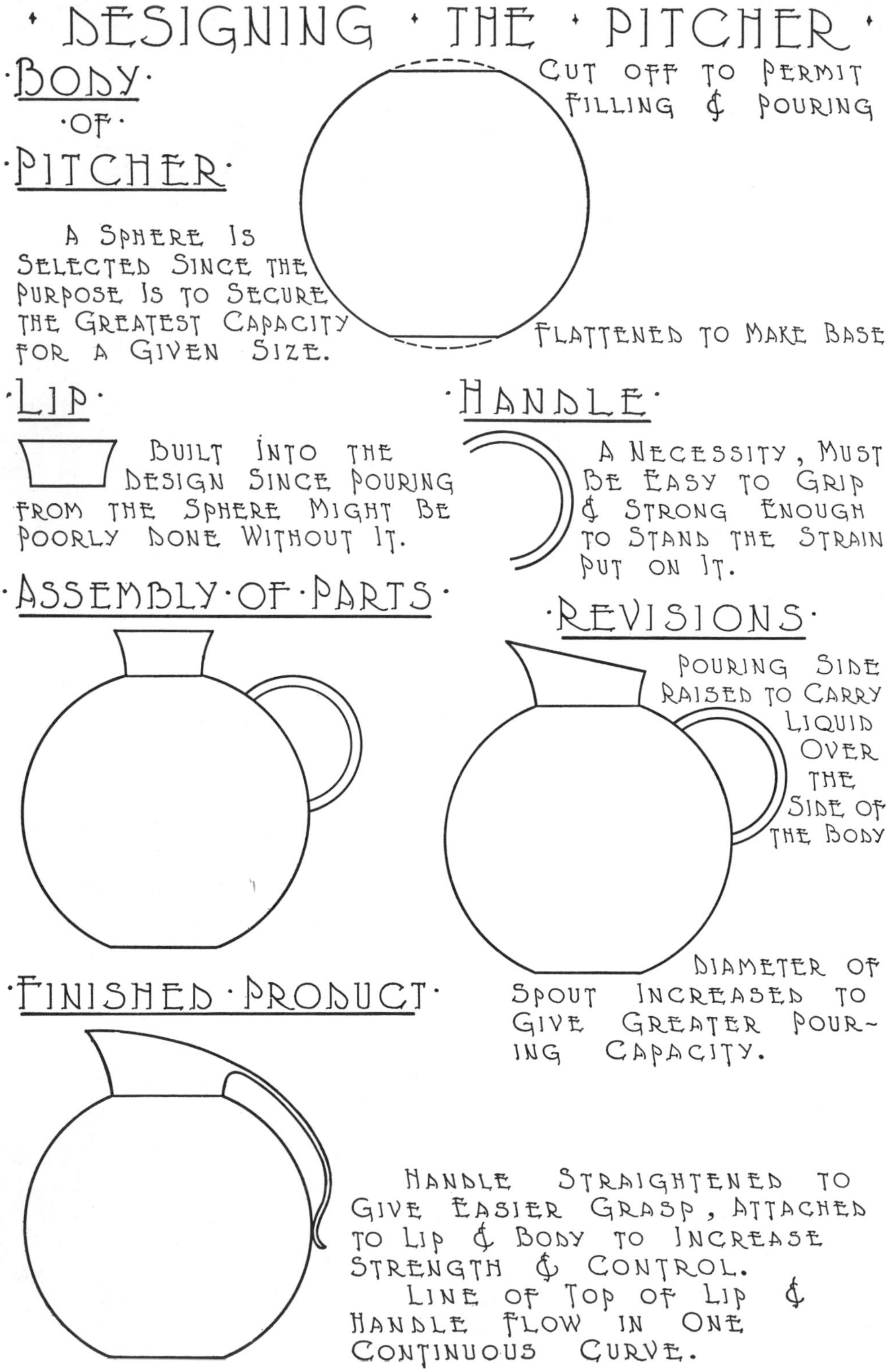

· DESIGNING · THE · PITCHER ·

·BODY· ·OF· ·PITCHER·

A SPHERE IS SELECTED SINCE THE PURPOSE IS TO SECURE THE GREATEST CAPACITY FOR A GIVEN SIZE.

CUT OFF TO PERMIT FILLING & POURING

FLATTENED TO MAKE BASE

·LIP·

BUILT INTO THE DESIGN SINCE POURING FROM THE SPHERE MIGHT BE POORLY DONE WITHOUT IT.

·HANDLE·

A NECESSITY, MUST BE EASY TO GRIP & STRONG ENOUGH TO STAND THE STRAIN PUT ON IT.

·ASSEMBLY·OF·PARTS·

·REVISIONS·

POURING SIDE RAISED TO CARRY LIQUID OVER THE SIDE OF THE BODY

·FINISHED·PRODUCT·

DIAMETER OF SPOUT INCREASED TO GIVE GREATER POURING CAPACITY.

HANDLE STRAIGHTENED TO GIVE EASIER GRASP, ATTACHED TO LIP & BODY TO INCREASE STRENGTH & CONTROL.

LINE OF TOP OF LIP & HANDLE FLOW IN ONE CONTINUOUS CURVE.

FIG. 27

When historic accuracy is desired, the designer should include all of the details of a piece, lest the omission of some of them may result in losing the desired effect. Usually he *should not attempt to compound a design* by using parts of one piece combined with the details of another. If the craftsman's technical skill is not equal to the task of making the piece in its entirety, a simpler article should be chosen, rather than to alter the more difficult one.

The designer who wishes to copy an original piece should first make a careful sketch of the entire article, giving each part as nearly its right proportion and true line as possible. Details may then be drawn and marked to identify their place on the whole piece. The drawing should be completed by measurement made with scale, calipers, dividers, curve-fitting gauges, or other useful tools. Since pewter is soft, extreme care must be taken not to scratch the surface with the measuring tools. Accuracy may be secured by making wax impressions of details, from which plaster casts can be made for further study, or for making plaster molds for casting pewter. Care should be observed in using wax not to bend the pewter when making the impression.

It should be recognized that an absolute copy cannot be made, but much of this unavoidable difference may be overcome by studying the method whereby the original ware was made, and by using the same method for reproduction. For instance, a hand-hammered piece cannot be reproduced accurately by spinning or casting, nor can the cast article be reproduced successfully by any other process. The quality of metal employed varied so widely in early ware that some experimentation becomes necessary when making accurate reproductions, to find a metal with an alloy close to that of the original.

The Functional Approach. Someone has said that an artist is one who enjoys a limitation. The successful designer of pewter ware should recognize the limitations of his material by not attempting to force it to uses or shapes unsuited to its character. The designer of original work should take into account the fact that the metal bends easily, and so plan to use a gauge sufficiently heavy to withstand the strains that will be applied to it. Handles, or other appendages, should be planned carefully in order to secure the necessary strength without creating an overbalanced effect. An examination of old ware will show that thin parts or sharp edges do not hold up. Pewter designers, therefore, should *avoid making sharp edges* or thin projecting parts in such a place as the joining of curves on round work; and by *holding decoration close to the surface,* instead of modeling it in high relief. Similarly, intricate design is inappropriate on pewter, since ordinary wear will destroy the details if they are very delicate. The low melting point of the metal excludes it from use for any article that must be heated over a stove.

· SURFACE · DECORATION ·

DECORATION · ARISING · FROM · MECHANICAL · FUNCTION

·PLATE·

BORDER ADDED
FOR ADDITIONAL STRENGTH

CURVATURE ADDED TO
STIFFEN THE RIM.
FIG. 28

·BEAKER·

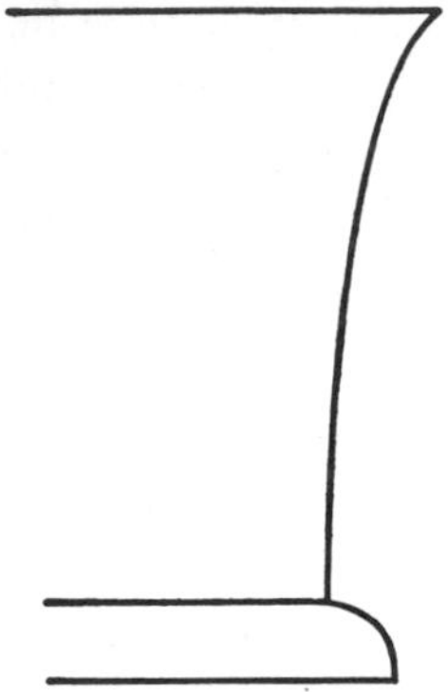

HEAVY FOOT ADDED TO
GIVE STABILITY & ADD
TO WEARING QUALITIES.
FIG. 31

LINE ENGRAVED
AROUND BODY TO COVER
SOLDERED JOINT AT POINT
OF GREATEST DIAMETER.
FIG. 32

·TEA-STRAINER·

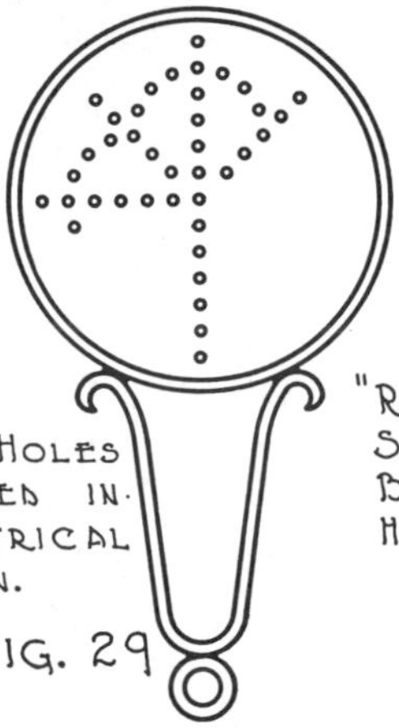

HOLES
ARRANGED IN
SYMMETRICAL
PATTERN.
FIG. 29

·VASE·

·TRAY·

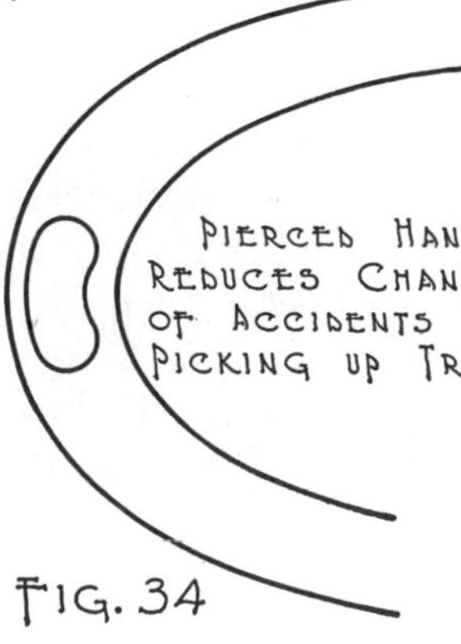

PIERCED HANDLE
REDUCES CHANCES
OF ACCIDENTS IN
PICKING UP TRAY.

FIG. 34

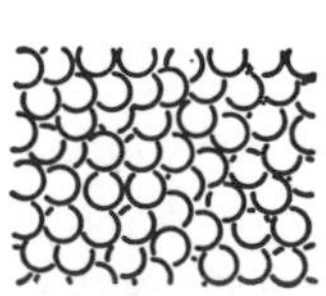

·RAT-TAIL · SPOON·

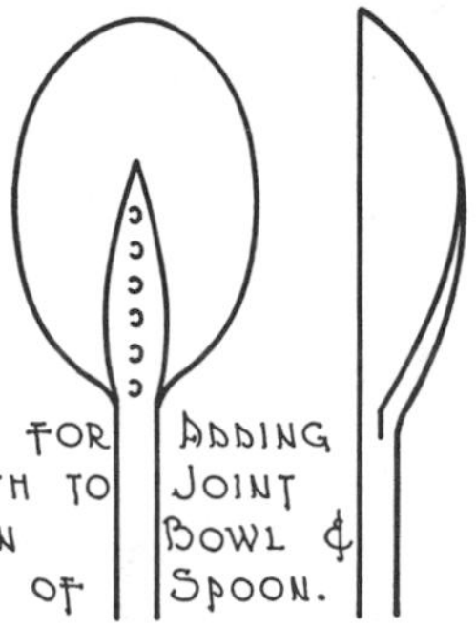

"RAT-TAIL" FOR ADDING
STRENGTH TO JOINT
BETWEEN BOWL &
HANDLE OF SPOON.
FIG. 30

FLUTED OR DOMED SURFACE
USED TO DIFFUSE LIGHT.
FIG. 33

PLANISHED SURFACE
DEVELOPED. BY
FORMING THE
ARTICLE. RAYS
OF LIGHT ARE
DIFFUSED, ADDING
TO INTEREST.
FIG. 35

HANDLE OF PORRINGER
PIERCED TO AID COOLING.
FIG.36

Because of these limitations, good pewter ware is usually plain and simple in design, harmonizing well with surroundings that are charming because of their quiet dignity. The texture and composition of the metal create a lovely sheen that is distinctive, and especially appropriate with unvarnished oak, pine, or maple furniture, and with hand-woven textiles.

The modern designer often attempts to abandon historic styles, and so create fresh designs. Such designs are usually based on a mechanical functional analysis of the desired article. This functional approach being free from stylistic restrictions, may devote itself solely to the utility of the article under consideration. The first step in designing is that of deciding just what the utensil is to do; then what features it must possess in order to carry out its purpose. The small pitcher, for instance, is designed with three necessary parts, body, lip, and handle, each of which serves a necessary use; the process of designing being set forth in detail in Fig. 27.

The second problem of the designer is that of planning the most useful structure and shape for each part. In the third step, the designer assembles these parts to secure the most effective use from each; at the same time arranging them, balancing proportions, and refining the lines. It must be realized, of course, that these steps are not entirely independent, but that all three must be kept in mind at one time.

As the illustration of the designing of the pitcher shows, good proportion is first of all a matter of the relative importance and use of the various parts. There is no safe rule to follow, other than that *each part shall have whatever size and shape best serves its purpose, when considered in its relation to other parts and the use of the entire object.* The success of the application of such a rule depends on the skill and good judgment of the designer, but it should be clear that there is no single solution to a designing problem.

The plainness and simplicity of good pewter demand a great deal of care in designing the outline or contour of any article. Outlines may be accented by emphasizing the strength of the line by means of adding a line or lines parallel to the contour, or by making the edge heavier. *Curves must flow smoothly,* avoiding sharp breaks or acute angle intersections. This rule is especially true in designing spun or hammered work in which it is impracticable to attempt to force the metal into sharp corners.

In general *the entire contour of an object should show lines of a similar character;* that is, either straight lines, arcs of circles (and other geometric forms), or free-hand curves, such as the natural curve of force. The *rate of curvature should also be kept constant* in one piece, so far as possible.

One immediate result of the functional approach to design is that *most ornament as such becomes illogical*, and a useless addition, unless it can earn its place by serving some useful purpose. It may perform such service by calling attention to some part, or by adding interest and attractiveness where it is needed. *Surface decoration* must be sparingly used, and *should grow out of the function*, or be the natural outgrowth of the method of making the piece. If this rule is observed, the decoration will be subordinated naturally to its proper degree of prominence.

The use of a border to stiffen the edge of plates, bowls, and similar utensils is shown in Fig. 28 while the symmetrical placement of holes in the tea strainer as shown in Fig. 29 adds beauty as well as utility. The peculiar handle construction used in the "rat-tail" spoon shown in Fig. 30 adds decoration and at the same time supports the point of greatest strain. The heavy foot on the beaker in Fig. 31 provides stability and adds to appearance. An engraved line is used on the vase shown in Fig. 32 to cover the necessary soldered joint, while the flutes on the sconce in Fig. 33 help to diffuse the light and add attractiveness. The same purpose is attained by planishing the surface of any article as indicated in Fig. 35. Two methods of using handles for decorative purposes are shown in Figs. 34 and 36.

· LAYING-OUT · AND · FORMING · TOOLS ·

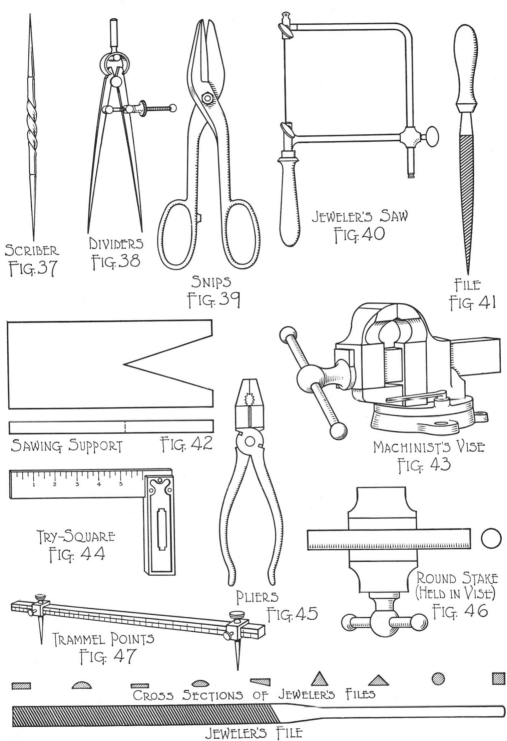

SCRIBER
FIG. 37

DIVIDERS
FIG. 38

SNIPS
FIG. 39

JEWELER'S SAW
FIG. 40

FILE
FIG 41

SAWING SUPPORT   FIG. 42

MACHINIST'S VISE
FIG. 43

TRY-SQUARE
FIG. 44

PLIERS
FIG. 45

ROUND STAKE
(HELD IN VISE)
FIG. 46

TRAMMEL POINTS
FIG. 47

CROSS SECTIONS OF JEWELER'S FILES

JEWELER'S FILE
FIG. 48

Chapter Four

Lay-Out and Forming

HE PEWTER CRAFTSMAN, with instruments and implements at hand as are shown in part in Figs. 37 to 48, will do well to draw a number of sketches of each article he proposes to make, changing each sketch until he is satisfied with the result. A detailed full-size working drawing should be made from the final approved sketch, and patterns developed where necessary.

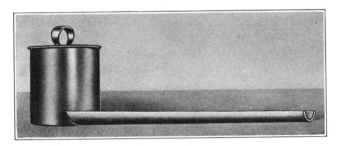

Fig. 49—Pen and Ink Holder

For example, the pen and ink holder (Fig. 49) should be drawn full size to whatever dimensions are decided upon. Patterns should be developed from this drawing for the ink bottle holder, the tray, the handle, and the cover rings, the details of the design of which are set forth in Figs. 50, 51, 52, and 53.

It will be noted that the development of the ink bottle cylinder is a simple rectangle which can be laid out directly on the sheet of metal by means of a rule, square, and scriber. If one edge of the metal is straight the body of the square may be placed against it and lines drawn along the blade. The same procedure may be followed for the other parts.

The ring handle is wider at the top, so that its pattern must be developed, cut out of paper, and pasted directly to the surface of the pewter. The lid and bottom of the ink-bottle holder are circles and may be drawn directly on the pewter by dividers whose points are set to the radii of the circles. Scribed lines drawn on the metal must be very light, as it is a difficult if not impossible task to remove them.

· DETAILS · OF · HOLDER ·

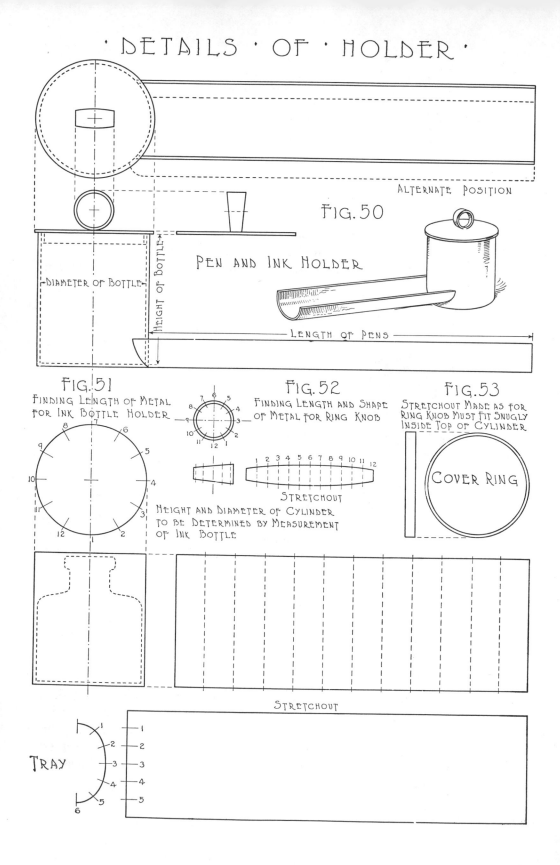

ALTERNATE POSITION

FIG. 50

PEN AND INK HOLDER

DIAMETER OF BOTTLE

HEIGHT OF BOTTLE

LENGTH OF PENS

FIG. 51
FINDING LENGTH OF METAL
FOR INK BOTTLE HOLDER

FIG. 52
FINDING LENGTH AND SHAPE
OF METAL FOR RING KNOB

STRETCHOUT

HEIGHT AND DIAMETER OF CYLINDER
TO BE DETERMINED BY MEASUREMENT
OF INK BOTTLE

FIG. 53
STRETCHOUT MADE AS FOR
RING KNOB MUST FIT SNUGLY
INSIDE TOP OF CYLINDER

COVER RING

STRETCHOUT

TRAY

· FASHIONING · THE · HOLDER ·

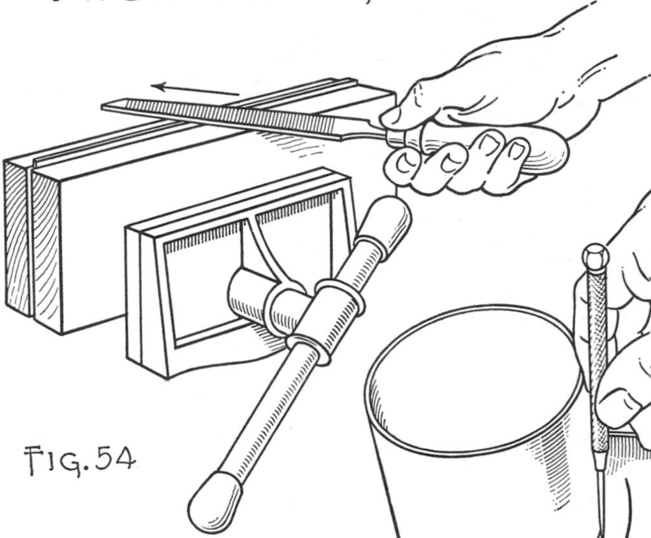

FIG.54

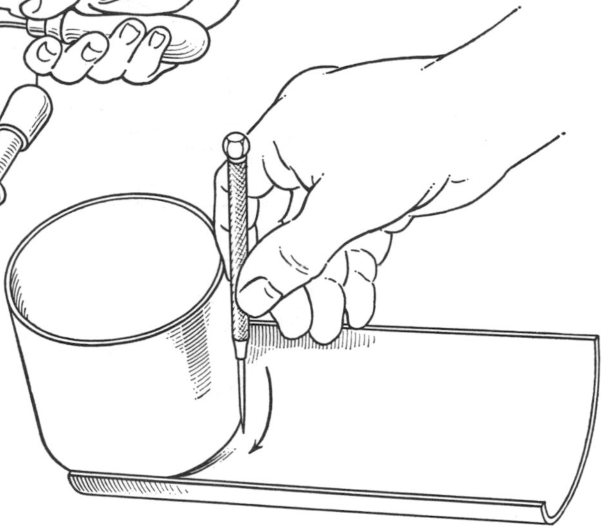

FIG.55

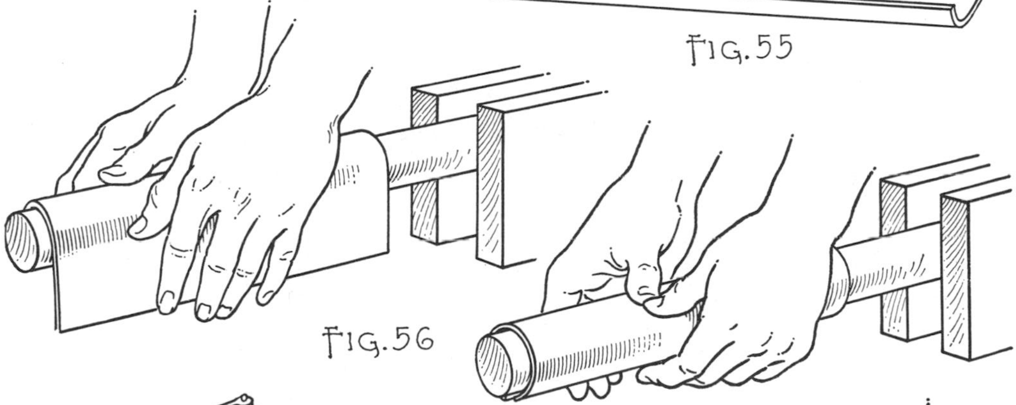

FIG.56

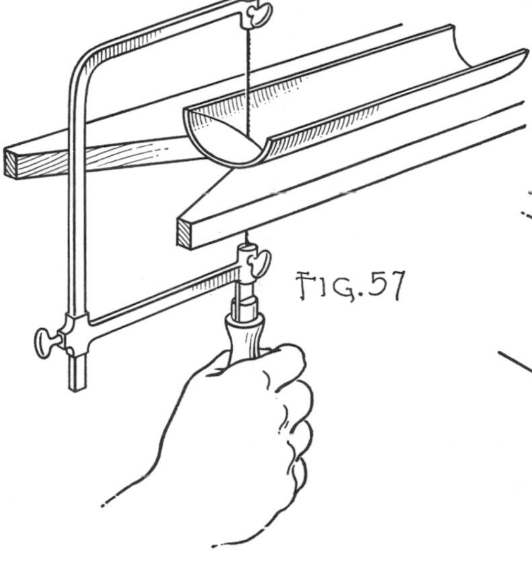

FIG.57

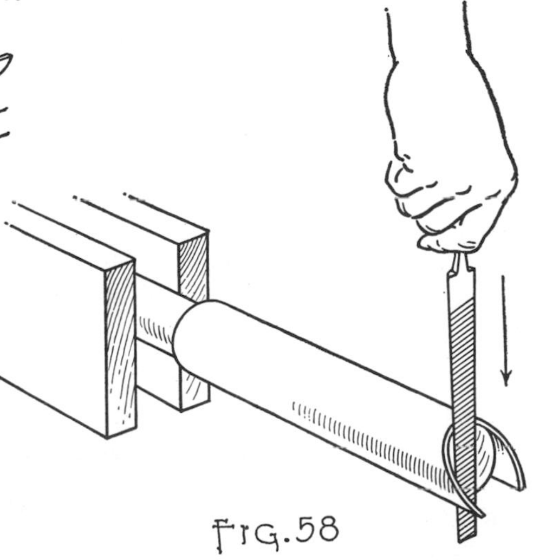

FIG.58

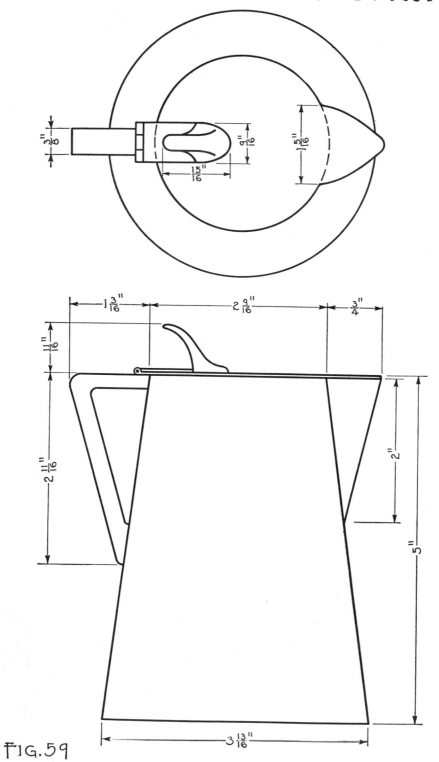

FIG. 59

· PATTERN · FOR · THE · SYRUP ·

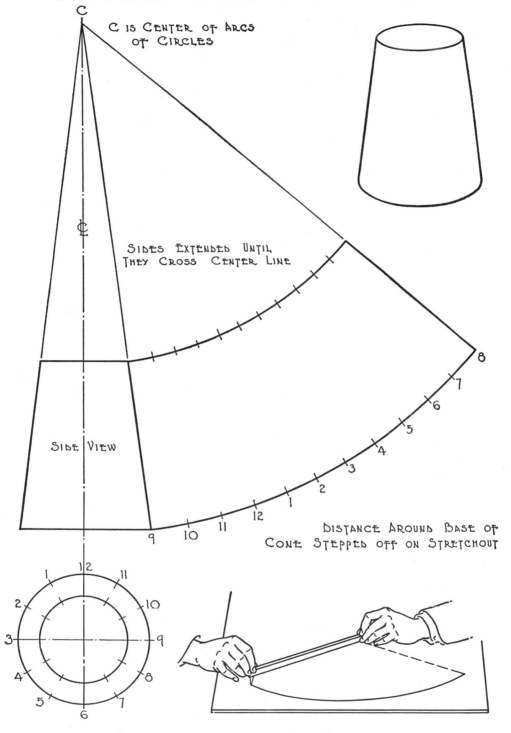

C IS CENTER OF ARCS
OF CIRCLES

SIDES EXTENDED UNTIL
THEY CROSS CENTER LINE

SIDE VIEW

DISTANCE AROUND BASE OF
CONE STEPPED OFF ON STRETCHOUT

· DEVELOPEMENT · OF · CONE ·
FIG. 60

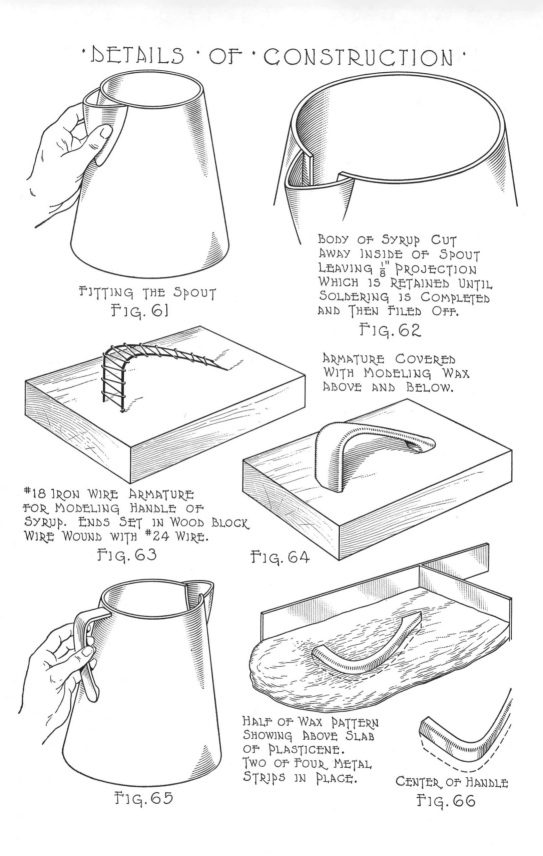

·DETAILS·OF·CONSTRUCTION·

FITTING THE SPOUT
FIG. 61

BODY OF SYRUP CUT
AWAY INSIDE OF SPOUT
LEAVING $\frac{1}{8}$" PROJECTION
WHICH IS RETAINED UNTIL
SOLDERING IS COMPLETED
AND THEN FILED OFF.
FIG. 62

ARMATURE COVERED
WITH MODELING WAX
ABOVE AND BELOW.

#18 IRON WIRE ARMATURE
FOR MODELING HANDLE OF
SYRUP. ENDS SET IN WOOD BLOCK
WIRE WOUND WITH #24 WIRE.
FIG. 63

FIG. 64

HALF OF WAX PATTERN
SHOWING ABOVE SLAB
OF PLASTICENE.
TWO OF FOUR METAL
STRIPS IN PLACE.

FIG. 65

CENTER OF HANDLE
FIG. 66

Sharp tinner's snips should be used to cut out the rectangular forms, keeping just outside the lines. Before cutting out the circles, enclose each in a square scribed tangent to it. Any attempt to cut a circle directly from a large piece of metal usually results in bending and spoiling much of the surrounding part. An economical procedure is to first cut out this square, cut off the corners about one-eighth inch from the circle, then trim to the finish line. All scraps should be saved for use in casting. If circle shears are available they are an efficient means of cutting true circles cleanly.

Each piece of metal should have all edges filed to the scribed lines. Thin metal must be supported to prevent bending or vibration. Clamp the metal in a vise between two smooth pieces of wood with about one-eighth inch projecting above the edge. File straight across the metal, using a six- or eight-inch second-cut file. Work from one end to the other and back, as indicated in Fig. 54, repeating until the metal is removed to the line. The file will clog easily with the soft metal, and must be kept scrupulously clean with a file card, otherwise the metal will become scratched.

After all filing is completed, the metal is shaped to the correct curvature over smooth stakes made of close-grained hard wood turned to the desired diameter. The shaping may be done with the hands by first curving the edges, then working each way to the center (Fig. 56). Secure the cylinder of metal with two or three lengths of binding wire so that the filed edges fit tightly, and the ends are even. Suspend the metal with the joint down (Fig. 81); add flux, and solder snippets. (See Chapter 5.) Set the soldered cylinder on the base, and hold down with a weight while soldering. (Fig. 82.)

Shape the pen holder, then hold the cylinder in position and scribe a line on the tray outlining the curve of the cylinder (Fig. 55). While sawing to this line (Fig. 57), rotate the tray so that the point being sawed is close to the support at all times. This sawed edge should be filed, using a fine half-round file until it will fit tightly against the curve of the cylinder (Fig. 58). It is a good plan to mark the place where the tray is to be fitted, otherwise a slight variation in curvature will make fitting difficult or impossible. The process of soldering is described in Chapter 5.

Syrup. Drawings for the "syrup" should be made as described for the pen and ink tray, as illustrated in Fig. 59. A pattern should be developed for the conical body, cut out, and rolled up into shape as a test of correctness. The method of developing this pattern is shown in Fig. 60. The lay-out may be made directly on the metal, using trammel points to scribe the arcs. The outside curve may be cut with a pair of "pivot" snips, but the inner one should be cut with a jeweler's saw. Shaping and wiring are done as before, except

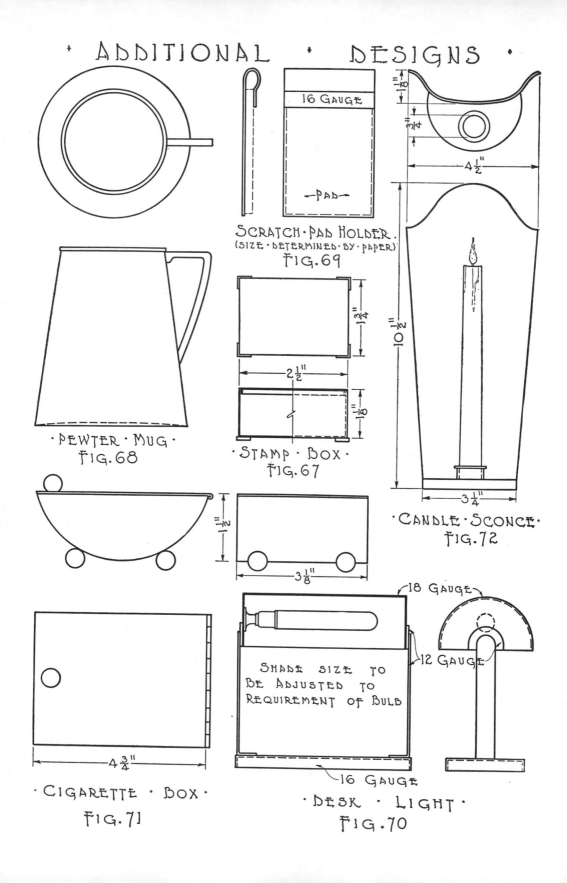

⋅ ADDITIONAL ⋅ DESIGNS ⋅

16 GAUGE

←PAD→

SCRATCH⋅PAD HOLDER⋅
(SIZE⋅DETERMINED⋅BY⋅PAPER)
FIG.69

⋅PEWTER⋅MUG⋅
FIG.68

$1\frac{3}{4}''$

$2\frac{1}{2}''$

$1\frac{1}{8}''$

⋅STAMP⋅BOX⋅
FIG.67

$1\frac{1}{8}''$

$\frac{3}{4}''$

$4\frac{1}{2}''$

$10\frac{1}{2}''$

$3\frac{1}{4}''$

⋅CANDLE⋅SCONCE⋅
FIG.72

$1\frac{1}{2}''$

$3\frac{1}{8}''$

18 GAUGE

12 GAUGE

SHADE SIZE TO
BE ADJUSTED TO
REQUIREMENT OF BULB

16 GAUGE

$4\frac{3}{4}''$

⋅CIGARETTE⋅BOX⋅
FIG.71

⋅DESK⋅LIGHT⋅
FIG.70

that vertical wires must be used to hold the horizontal ones in place (see Fig. 85).

After soldering the joint, true up the body on a stake until the base will closely fit a circle drawn to the diameter shown on the working drawing. Fold a piece of heavy paper and cut to the approximate shape and size of the spout. Alter this pattern by trial until it fits the body of the cone (Fig. 61), then paste onto a piece of pewter and saw to shape. The spout should be filed and tested until a tight joint is secured, then the body cut away inside the spout almost to the inner edge (Fig. 62).

Cut out the circular piece for the bottom, leaving about one-eighth inch extra projecting around the bottom for soldering. Model the pattern for the handle out of wax which should be formed around a wire frame or armature, and fitted in place on the cone or pitcher body to test its size and proportion (Figs. 63, 64, 65, and 66).

Wire the bottom spout and handle in place and solder as described in Chapter 5. Trim and file away all metal left projecting for soldering purposes.

Turn the finished body upside down on a piece of metal and scribe around the top and spout. Cut out this piece and mount on it the upper leaf of the hinge and the thumb piece which has been cast from a wax pattern.

Polishing should be done by hand, using fine or No. 00 steel wool, then tripoli and oil on a soft cloth, followed by rouge or silver polish. Rubbing should always be done in the direction of the natural lines of the object.

The stamp box (Fig. 67), the mug (Fig. 68), the scratch-pad holder (Fig. 69), the desk light (Fig. 70), the cigarette box (Fig. 71), and the candle sconce (Fig. 72), all provide interesting ideas in pewter ware involving similar processes and techniques.

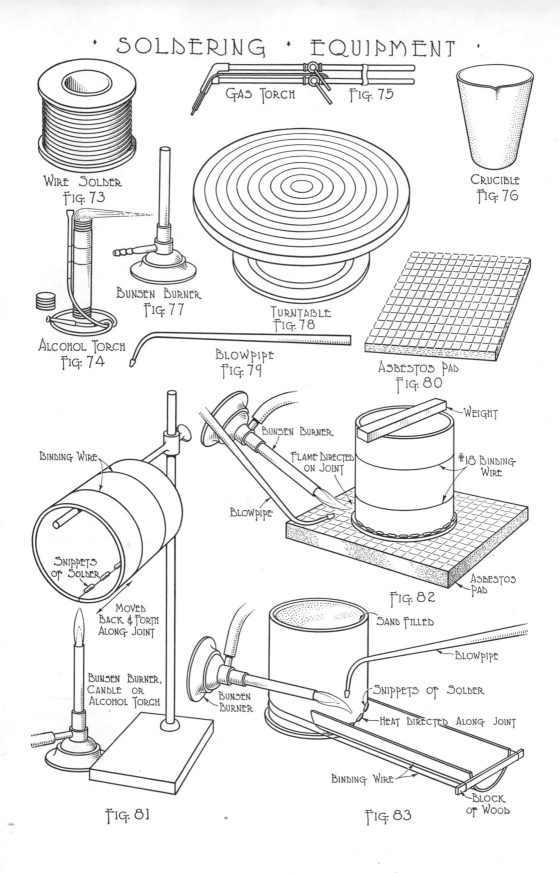

· SOLDERING · EQUIPMENT ·

GAS TORCH   FIG. 75

WIRE SOLDER
FIG. 73

CRUCIBLE
FIG. 76

BUNSEN BURNER
FIG. 77

TURNTABLE
FIG. 78

ALCOHOL TORCH
FIG. 74

BLOWPIPE
FIG. 79

ASBESTOS PAD
FIG. 80

BINDING WIRE

BUNSEN BURNER

FLAME DIRECTED
ON JOINT

BLOWPIPE

WEIGHT

#18 BINDING
WIRE

SNIPPETS
OF SOLDER

MOVED
BACK & FORTH
ALONG JOINT

ASBESTOS
PAD

FIG. 82

BUNSEN BURNER,
CANDLE OR
ALCOHOL TORCH

BUNSEN
BURNER

SAND FILLED

BLOWPIPE

SNIPPETS OF SOLDER

HEAT DIRECTED ALONG JOINT

BINDING WIRE

BLOCK
OF WOOD

FIG. 81

FIG. 83

Chapter Five

Soldering

*A*MOST important property of pewter relates to the ease with which it may be soldered. The fact that pewter contains a large percentage of tin (one of the constituent parts of solder) makes the joining process so complete that it is difficult to detect where the edges of the metal have been united. One of the first requisites for soldering is a source of heat. Several alternatives are available. An ordinary bunsen burner (Fig. 77), an alcohol torch (Fig. 74), or a candle may be used. All of these require a mouth-type blow pipe (Fig. 79) to direct the point of the flame; or a small gas torch (Fig. 75) connected with compressed air may be used. It should be remembered that *pewter should never be soldered by use of a soldering copper*. The concentration of heat caused by touching the point of the copper to the pewter is almost sure to melt a hole through it. A turntable (Fig. 78) may be used to advantage for certain types of work, and is especially adaptable where two cylindrical pieces are soldered together. A further accessory is one or more asbestos pads (Fig. 80). These pads are essential as a means of support for small pieces.

If extensive work in soldering is contemplated several types of solder should be secured, permitting the making of successive joints on a single project without fear of melting those previously soldered. For some types of work snippets of the pewter itself are recommended. These melt at the same temperature as pewter (425-440° F.). They should be used however, only after considerable experience in soldering has been gained, and after trials on scrap pieces. The same precautions hold for the use of 50-50 solder, which is sometimes used for the first joint, and which melts at 370° F. A type of solder more suited to pewter work is 60-40, which contains 60 parts of tin and 40 parts of lead and which melts at about 340° F. If one wishes the very lowest melting solder of any lead and tin mixture he should secure the 63-37 type. This mixture is known as "eutectic" solder and is the kind commonly purchased if only one is desired. A type which melts still lower, however, is an alloy of lead, tin, and bismuth, known as bismuth solder, which may be used where special precautions against melting the pewter are necessary.

The soldering of pewter requires the use of a flux to prevent the metal from oxidation and to make the solder flow more freely. The most commonly used flux is composed of glycerine with about 10 drops of hydrochloric acid added to each ounce. Several commercial pewter fluxes which seem to give excellent results are also available. The flux should be liberally applied to the joints so that all parts are covered. It should be noted, however, that solder has a tendency to follow the flux and hence it should be placed with care.

Binding wire is also necessary. Joints must be securely wired in place, otherwise the action of heat will cause them to open or move out of place. Soft iron wire in sizes 18 and 24 is commonly used.

Joining the seam of the ink bottle holder described in Chapter 4, presents an interesting type of soldering as may be noted in Fig. 81. It is much safer for the beginner to experiment with a smaller piece of scrap pewter before attempting the actual job. Cut out a piece of scrap in the form of a ring about an inch wide and the same in diameter. Fasten with binding wire as described in Chapter 4, and support by slipping over a dowel held in a horizontal position from the vise jaws. Coat the inside of the seam with a liberal amount of glycerine-acid flux and place two or three snippets of 60-40 or 63-37 solder at the seam. The bunsen burner, alcohol lamp, or candle should then be passed back and forth on the underside of the joint. *Keep the flame moving constantly.* If it is allowed to stay in one spot for even an instant the metal is likely to melt. The flux will soon start to boil and very shortly afterwards the solder will melt and run into the joint. It is a well-known fact that the solder runs toward the hottest part of the metal. Since the heat is from below, the solder will be drawn completely through the joint and a perfect connection should result.

When the trial piece is successfully joined the same procedure should be applied to the cylinder which has previously been wired, as shown in Fig. 81. Be liberal in the use of flux in order that it will permeate the joint. Place the snippets of solder about half an inch apart and apply the heat as before. The heat should be removed when the solder has melted and flowed the full length of the seam. After the joint has cooled sufficiently for handling, the binding wire should be removed, and any excess solder removed with a second-cut file. The final cleaning of the joint may be accomplished by the use of fine (00) emery cloth. Care should be taken to polish lengthwise of the cylinder, and avoid scratching the work.

Another method of soldering is involved in joining the bottom to the cylinder. As described in Chapter 4, the bottom is cut slightly larger than the cylinder and is placed as in Fig. 82. Flux is applied liberally to the joint and snippets of solder placed around the outside. The work should be weighted from above and the bunsen burner or other source of heat rotated around the edge. The flux will soon boil and the solder melt into the joint. The projecting edge of the bottom may be cut as close to the side of the cylinder as practicable with the snips and then filed flush with the edge. The joint may then be smoothed with fine emery cloth.

The direct method of soldering is required in joining the tray to the ink bottle holder. The pieces should be fastened securely by placing a block of wood across the end of the tray and passing a wire around the cylinder as shown in Fig. 83. The cylinder should be filled with sand to avoid overheating the joints already soldered. Place the flux on the joint *inside* the tray, then the snippets of solder. Bring the lighted burner above the tray, being careful not to hold it too close to the cylinder. Direct the flame upon the joint with a blow pipe and move the point of heat continuously along the joint. Remove the flame as soon as the solder is fully melted.

Fig. 84—Pewter Syrup, made by Tom Ernest Moore

The seam of the side of the syrup (Fig. 84) should be soldered by following the procedure described for the ink bottle holder. The bottom, handle, and spout should then be wired in place as shown in Fig. 85, and all joints thoroughly fluxed. Solder the bottom as by the direct method shown in Fig. 82, then partly fill the cone with sand before soldering the spout. Completely fill with sand and solder the handle, using 50-50 solder. Make certain that the handle is straight and exactly opposite the spout before applying the heat.

· SOLDERING · SYRUP ·

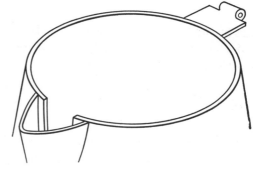

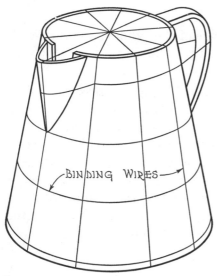

BINDING WIRES

SYRUP WIRED FOR SOLDERING
FIG. 85

SOLDERING OF HINGE TO SYRUP

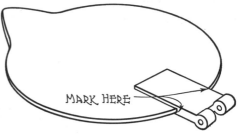

MARK HERE

FIG. 86

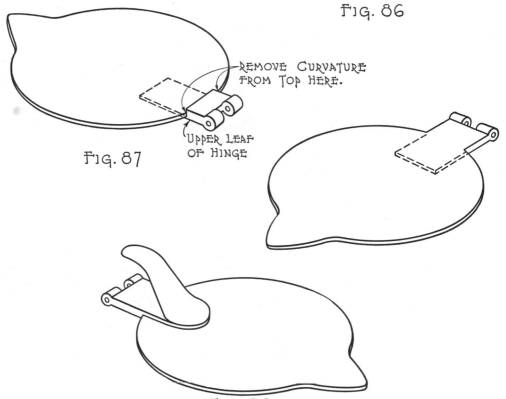

REMOVE CURVATURE
FROM TOP HERE.

UPPER LEAF
OF HINGE

FIG. 87

FIG. 88

The bottom part of the hinge should be fitted to the curvature of the top and soldered just above the handle with a 63-37 solder as illustrated in Figs. 85, 86, 87, and 88. If care is used in applying the heat this operation should not disturb the 50-50 solder used on the handle. The top of the syrup and the top part of the hinge should be placed in position and the points where the edge of the top passes under the hinge carefully marked (see Fig. 86). The under part of the hinge should be filed away so that it will be flush with the under side of the top. The curvature on that part of the top which is under the hinge may be cut away to make the fitting easier (Fig. 87). Small wire clamps similar to those used in reeding should be used to hold the hinge in place while the heat is applied. Use 50-50 solder and apply the flame mainly to the hinge, allowing the heat to travel toward the lighter metal of the top. The bottom of the thumb piece should be filed until it is flat and is at the correct angle with the top (Fig. 88). Apply flux and 63-37 solder, then, keeping the flame mainly upon the heavy metal of the thumb piece, melt the solder by the direct method. All joints on the syrup should be filed and cleaned as described above in preparation for the final polish.

Chapter Six

Plaster Casting

$\mathcal{P}$EWTER is an ideal metal for making small castings because it melts at such a low temperature and flows so easily. The antimony contained in the alloy adds to the sharpness of detail by preventing shrinkage, while the high tin content prevents excessive oxidation of the finished article. Plaster seems best suited as a medium for making molds where a good finish is desired with maximum detail and only one or two castings of a given kind are needed.

This type of casting requires but little equipment not found in the average school or home shop. Pieces of glass of different sizes are convenient as a surface upon which to do the molding. Strips of tin plate or galvanized iron of various widths and lengths are needed as side pieces for forms. A dish (if possible a round-bottomed bowl) and two or three sizes of spoons (wood preferred) are used for mixing the plaster. Several common shapes and sizes of modeling tools for making wax patterns and smoothing wax surfaces are desirable but not absolutely essential.

The necessary supplies include some form of modeling wax or clay. The plasticene commonly used for simple modeling is recommended. This material may be purchased at toy or school supply stores.

Fig. 89—Ship's Candlestick

Plaster of Paris in two grades should also be secured. A few pounds of dental plaster, which is very fine and gives excellent detail, should be at hand for covering the face of the patterns, in addition to a larger amount of ordinary finishing plaster for backing up the facing and giving body to the mold.

The Ship's Candlestick. The making of the Ship's Candlestick shown in Fig. 89 involves most of the processes usually considered in connection with plaster casting. These processes should be applicable not only to this particular project, but to any others of a similar character.

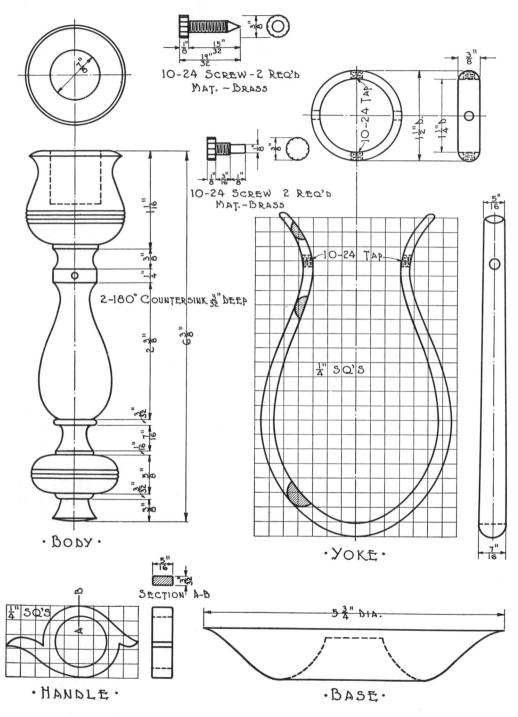

$\frac{7}{8}$"

10-24 SCREW-2 REQ'D
MAT. ~ BRASS

$\frac{1}{8}$" $\frac{15}{32}$"
$\frac{19}{32}$"
$\frac{3}{8}$"

10-24 TAP

$\frac{3}{8}$"

$1\frac{1}{2}$ D. $1\frac{1}{4}$ D.

$\frac{5}{16}$"

10-24 SCREW 2 REQ'D
MAT. ~ BRASS

$\frac{1}{8}$" $\frac{3}{16}$" $\frac{1}{8}$"

$\frac{3}{8}$"

$1\frac{1}{16}$"

$\frac{3}{8}$"

$1\frac{1}{4}$"

2-180° COUNTERSINK $\frac{3}{32}$" DEEP

$2\frac{3}{8}$"

$6\frac{3}{8}$"

10-24 TAP

$\frac{1}{4}$" SQ'S

$\frac{3}{32}$"

$\frac{7}{16}$"

$1\frac{1}{16}$"

$\frac{5}{8}$"

$\frac{3}{32}$"

$\frac{3}{8}$"

· BODY ·

· YOKE ·

$\frac{7}{16}$"

$\frac{5}{16}$"

$\frac{3}{32}$"
SECTION A-B

$\frac{1}{4}$ SQ'S

B

A

· HANDLE ·

$5\frac{3}{4}$" DIA.

· BASE ·

· DETAILS · OF · SHIP'S · CANDLESTICK ·
FIG. 90

The pattern for the stem should be made first. Two pieces of pine or mahogany 1 in. × 2 in. × 8½ in. should be secured and squared accurately to size. Lay out carefully the locations for the dowels on the face of one piece as shown in Fig. 91. These dowels should be so placed that they will come in the large parts of the finished pattern. At each of these points drive a small brad and clip off the head about $\frac{1}{16}$ inch from the surface of the wood. If the second piece is now placed in position above the first and the two pressed together the brads will mark the position for the dowel holes. Remove the brads and drill $\frac{3}{16}$-inch holes in each piece about $\frac{5}{16}$ of an inch deep. In one piece insert $\frac{3}{16}$ in. × ½ in. brass dowels and enlarge the holes in the other until they will drop apart by their own weight.

The two pieces should now be glued together with a piece of heavy paper in the joint. When dry locate the center point on each end, being sure that it comes on the joint between the two pieces. Mount in the lathe and turn to the shape and size shown in Fig. 90. A template made from cardboard, veneer stock, or sheet metal will aid in securing the correct shapes. It should be noted that a plug is left on each end of this pattern so that the casting may be mounted in the lathe for cleaning up. Careful sanding should be followed by several coats of shellac before removal from the lathe. The heavy paper may be split with a razor blade or sharp chisel allowing the pattern to come apart.

The pattern for the U-shaped support may be made from either wood or metal. The one shown in Fig. 96 was made from a piece of half-round brass. The length was first determined by bending a strip of sheet metal to fit the lines of the full-sized drawing, and the brass filed to correct shape (as shown by the sections Fig. 90). The material was then annealed by heating, and carefully bent to conform to the drawing. Two metal pins held in a vise and padded with paper served as a bending device and prevented marring the metal.

If a wooden pattern is used, material of the correct thickness should be band- or jig-sawed to the correct shape (Fig 92), then the correct section obtained by use of a spoke-shave, files, and sand paper. Finally, sand the surface smooth and give several coats of shellac.

The pattern for the ring (Fig. 93) may be made in either of two ways. It may take the form of the ring or it may be a straight piece having a half-round section, in which case the metal is bent to form the ring after it is cast, and soldered together. The pattern in either case is best made of wood, and it should be shellacked to preserve it from moisture.

The pattern for the handle (Fig. 94) should be made of wood. Lay out the full-sized outline on the face of a piece of mahogany ⅜ of an inch thick and

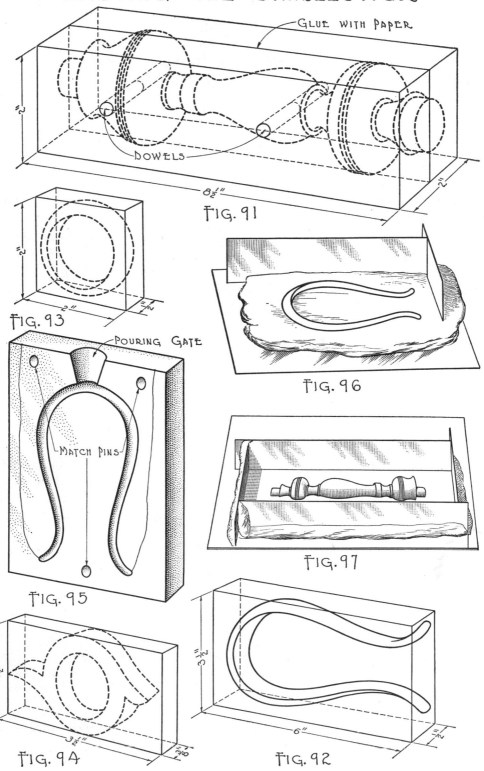

· CASTING · THE · CANDLESTICK ·

GLUE WITH PAPER

DOWELS

FIG. 91

FIG. 93

POURING GATE

MATCH PINS

FIG. 95

FIG. 96

FIG. 97

FIG. 94

FIG. 92

saw carefully on the outside of the lines. Drill a small hole on the part which is to be cut away for the inside; insert a jig- or coping-saw blade, and saw out the inner portion. A jack knife or file may be used to bring the blank to the correct section, and then it may be smoothed with sandpaper. When finished, apply several coats of shellac.

Making the Molds. The molds for this project may be made in either plaster or sand. For purposes of illustration the use of plaster molds is here described. The procedure described in Chapter 10 should be followed if it is desired to make sand molds.

The first step in the making of a plaster mold is to secure a suitable surface upon which to work. A piece of glass (ordinary window glass will do) at least 4 inches longer and 4 inches wider than the desired mold makes an excellent foundation. Two pieces of sheet metal 2 in. $\times$ 5 in. and two pieces 2 in. $\times$ 10 in. are required in making a mold for the body of the candlestick. Also secure a supply of plasticene and work it well in the hands until it is thoroughly pliable. This should then be rolled out into long rolls about $\frac{1}{2}$-inch in diameter.

Apply a thin film of cup grease on the flat side of the pattern which does not have the dowels, and place it with the flat side down upon the glass. The grease tends to hold the pattern in place and keeps it from shifting when the plaster is poured. Place the strips of sheet metal around the pattern with the ends overlapping as shown in Fig. 97, and fasten along the entire lower edges with the rolls of plasticene. Seal the corners of the box where the pieces meet. The box formed by the strips should be of such a size that there will be at least 2 inches between the top end of the candlestick and the edge of the mold, and at least $\frac{1}{2}$ an inch on all other sides.

The next step is mixing the plaster. Secure a dish of suitable size and shape, filling it with an amount of water which it is estimated will fill the mold to a depth of $\frac{1}{2}$ an inch over the largest part of the pattern. To this slowly add plaster of Paris in the center of the bowl, and continue until the water will absorb no more plaster and there is a mound of plaster in the center above the water as graphically described in Fig. 98. Then with a spoon or with the fingers mix the plaster thoroughly with the water. This operation should give a mixture of the consistency of thick cream, which forms an opaque coating over the spoon or fingers. If it does not attain this thickness, but seems too thin, add more plaster until the desired consistency is secured. The greatest care should be taken not to introduce air bubbles when mixing, therefore the stirring should be done below the surface of the mixture.

Pour the plaster into the mold as in Fig. 99, *jarring the solution continually to remove air bubbles* and to level the surface. If the plaster is mixed to

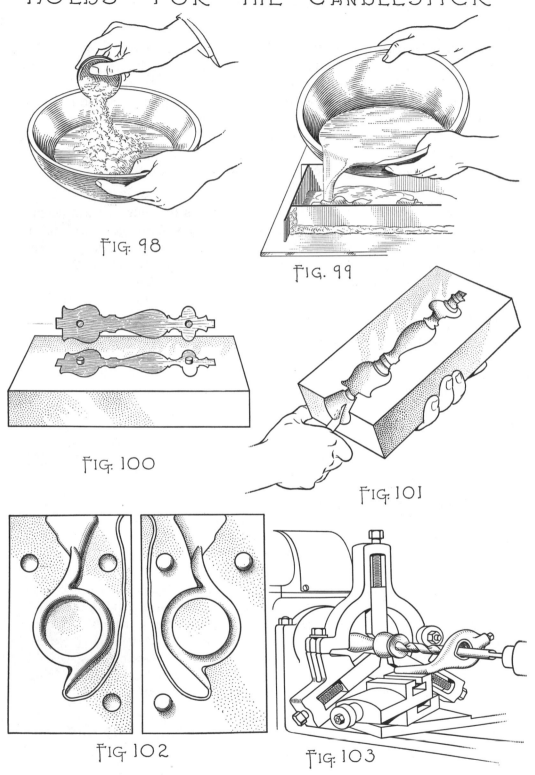

·MOLDS · FOR · THE · CANDLESTICK·

FIG. 98

FIG. 99

FIG. 100

FIG. 101

FIG. 102

FIG. 103

the right consistency it should start to harden almost at once, and should be hard enough to handle in fifteen to twenty minutes. If the mixture fails to "set" it is either because the plaster is of poor quality or the mixture too thin. All excess plaster left in the bowl or on the spoons should be rinsed off *immediately* in a pail of water. *In no case should plaster be allowed to enter the sink or other plumbing fixtures.* Where a great amount of this work is contemplated a plaster trap should be installed below the sink, which will separate anything apt to clog the drains.

After the first part of the mold is hard enough to handle, the strips of sheet metal and plasticene are removed, and the cast turned so that the pattern is upward. Examine it carefully and if the pattern is below the surface because the plaster has run under it, the surplus should be carefully scraped away until the face of the cast is even with the edge of the pattern. Several shallow, round holes should be made in the surface of the mold to form match pins when the top part is poured. Coat the surface which is to come in contact with the new plaster with a soap sizing, prepared by dissolving soap in hot water until a thick creamy mass is obtained. In the absence of this material, ordinary liquid soap has been found to give satisfactory results.

The second part of the pattern should be placed in position and sheet metal strips which are slightly wider than those used before, replaced and fastened with plasticene (Fig. 100). A new batch of plaster should be prepared and poured as before, being sure to bring the top surface at least half an inch above the highest part of the pattern. Allow the plaster to remain until hard, then remove the metal form. Rap the outside of the mold slightly and separate the two parts by inserting a knife blade or other thin instrument between the sections. Since the pattern is of wood allow the mold to dry before attempting to remove it. Rapping the patterns will often loosen them and make their removal easier.

Cut the pouring gate at the top end of the mold as shown in Fig. 101. Small vents for the escape of any trapped air should also be made from the lower end of the mold. These vents should not be large enough to allow the metal to flow through, and it is advisable in some cases to bring them up to the top of the mold to make sure that the metal will not drain out and ruin the casting (see Fig. 102). The mold should now be thoroughly dried. To dry them the separate halves should be laid near to or upon the top of a furnace, radiator, or other source of heat, and allowed to remain for several days. Avoid overheating during this drying process as the mold will warp, causing it to break when the parts are clamped together.

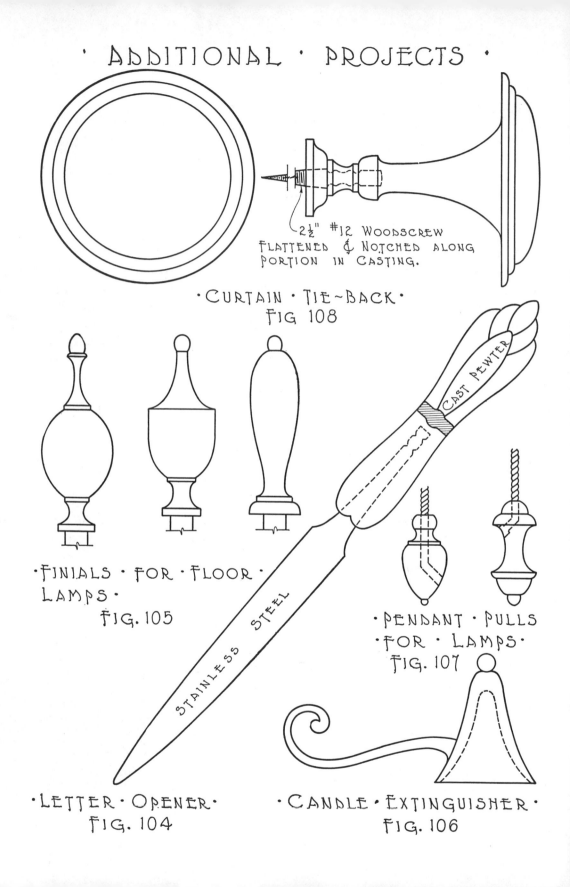

· ADDITIONAL · PROJECTS ·

2½" #12 WOODSCREW
FLATTENED & NOTCHED ALONG
PORTION IN CASTING.

· CURTAIN · TIE~BACK ·
FIG 108

CAST PEWTER

· FINIALS · FOR · FLOOR ·
LAMPS ·
FIG. 105

STAINLESS STEEL

· PENDANT · PULLS ·
FOR · LAMPS ·
FIG. 107

· LETTER · OPENER ·
FIG. 104

· CANDLE · EXTINGUISHER ·
FIG. 106

The mold for the U-shaped support requires a slightly different treatment. A piece of plasticene should be rolled out about half an inch thick and somewhat larger than the pattern. The pattern is pressed into this pad up to the center or parting line as shown in Fig. 96. The metal strips are placed around the pattern as in the case of the stem and the plaster is poured. When the plaster sets, cut the mold free from the glass by drawing a fine wire between them, then peel the plasticene away from the plaster. It is usually wise to remove the pattern before making the second part of the mold, and if the plaster is found to be above the parting line at any point, it should be carefully smoothed down with a sharp knife. Replace the pattern; make the necessary matching holes; soap size the top surface, and pour the second part of the mold. Fig. 95 shows how the gate and vents should be placed for this part.

The molds for the ring and for the handle are made in exactly the same manner as for the support. Fig. 102 shows the molds for the handle with the casting in place. Note the blackened surface due to the coating of carbon. This carbon provides a smoother casting.

When the molds are ready for pouring, coat the inside surface by smoking it over a lighted candle or gas flame, after which the parts should be tied together with a strong cord. The pewter should be heated in a ladle until it will slightly char a pine stick. If the mold is large, it should be held in a vise while the metal is poured. If it is small, however, it is usually better to hold it with a cloth, being sure that the fingers are not in a position to come in contact with any metal which may be spilled. If the mold is tilted to one side and gradually raised as the hot metal enters, the danger of trapping air within is diminished.

The stem of the candlestick is the only part that requires finishing on the lathe, and even this process may be unnecessary if the casting is very clean. The plugs at the end should be carefully centered and countersunk. Mount between lathe centers, and with ordinary wood turning tools true up the outside surface. The fine beads at the top and bottom are best renewed with a diamond point tool or with a metal working tool bit ground to a sharp point. When the correct shape is attained remove all tool marks with fine emery cloth. If cup grease is used on the work the danger of scratching the surface is minimized. The plug at the top should now be cut off, and the small plug held in a drill chuck placed in the head stock of the lathe. The stem should be supported in a steady rest on the flat part just below the bowl (Fig. 103 illustrates the operation). Adjust until the center point of the candlestick runs true with the tail stock center. Spot the center with a sharp pointed tool, and then using successively larger drills enlarge the candle socket to $\frac{7}{8}$ of an inch. The depth should be about 1 inch. Make sure at this point that all necessary polishing has been done, then cut off the plug at the lower end, and file the stem smooth. The final polishing should be done on the buffing wheel using first tripoli and then rouge. If a polishing lathe is not available, a buffing wheel mounted between the centers of an ordinary wood lathe will serve.

The remaining parts do not as a rule require machining. Rough spots may be removed with the file, after which steel wool and the buffing wheel should produce a suitable surface.

Directions for spinning the base are given in Chapter 11. In order that it may not seem too light for the heavy top parts, the metal should be not thinner than 16-gauge.

Assembling the Candlestick. Divide the outside of the ring into four equal parts and prick punch at these points for drilling. Two opposite points should be drilled with a No. 25 tap drill for the 10-24 machine screw threads. The other two points should be drilled with a No. 30 drill to receive the $\frac{1}{8}$-inch pilots of the shorter screws. Next drill a small pilot hole in the support at the points indicated with about a No. 40 drill and gradually increase the size of the holes with larger drills until the No. 25 is reached. Tap the two holes in the ring and those in the support with a 10-24 or a $\frac{3}{16}$-24 tap. It is important that the tap be held to bring the threads exactly horizontal, otherwise the stem will not pivot easily.

The screws should be made of brass according to the sketch in Fig. 90. Small grooves are filed in the heads to more nearly simulate the hand-made screws used in the original. When completed they should be dipped in zinc chloride and then in melted pewter. The threads will need to be recut and the heads lightly buffed after this treatment. The pivot holes in the stem which receive the ends of the screws should be drilled with a 60 degree countersink.

The support should now be slightly flattened at the bottom and adjusted until it stands exactly upright when placed upon the spun base. The soldering should be done by the direct method as described in Chapter 5 using a 63-37 solder and keeping the heat directed upon the heavy metal of the support. The handle should be accurately fitted to the base and soldered into place using the same technique.

All parts should be given a final polish with rouge or crocus, and the stem of the candlestick hung in place.

The method of casting handles, feet, and similar appendages from wax patterns may be illustrated by describing the process of making a handle for the syrup considered in Chapter 4 (Figs. 63-66). After the wax is modeled to the desired contour, the ends of the armature wires are carefully pulled out of their supports and clipped off close to the surface of the wax. A light line is drawn around the center to mark the parting line. Strips of plasticene cut to fit the outline of the handle are pressed into place so their top surface is in line with the parting line of the handle. The pattern is then laid upon a piece of glass; more plasticene placed under the strips to make them even, and the mold completed as in the case of the support for the candlestick.

The student may find suggestions for experimentation in casting pewter in the illustrations of the letter-opener handle, Fig. 104; the finials for floor lamps, Fig. 105; the candle extinguisher, Fig. 106; the pendent pulls for lamps, Fig. 107; and the curtain tie-back, Fig. 108.

Chapter Seven

Beating Down and Planishing

$\mathcal{M}$ANY ARTICLES cannot be made by a simple bending process, such as has been described, but must be formed by hammering the metal into shape. Tools and accessories for thus fashioning pewter are shown in Figs. 109 to 119.

A rather simple method is by beating down portions of the metal, as on a plate or tray, Figs. 120 to 126. For this kind of work pewter is best laid on the end of a close-grained hardwood block, which has been planed and sanded.

Fig. 127—Oval Tray

To make the tray (Fig. 127), draw two ellipses (Fig. 135), to the desired size on a piece of paper. These ellipses may be drawn by using a string as a radius, with major and minor axes (Fig. 131). The rim of the tray is widened slightly at the ends to form the handles. Paste this pattern to the metal and cut with the snips about one-quarter inch outside the pattern (Fig. 132). This extra metal is left to offset the drawing-in effect of beating down, since the rim will tend to become narrowed under the blows of the forming hammer. The inner guide line should be marked by lightly cutting through the paper with a sharp knife along the line of the inner ellipse. This guide line indicates where the beating down is to be done.

Remove the pattern and planish the area within the inner guide line by covering it with closely-laid hammer blows, as illustrated by Fig. 134. For this process lay the metal on the flat hardwood stake and hold it with one hand.

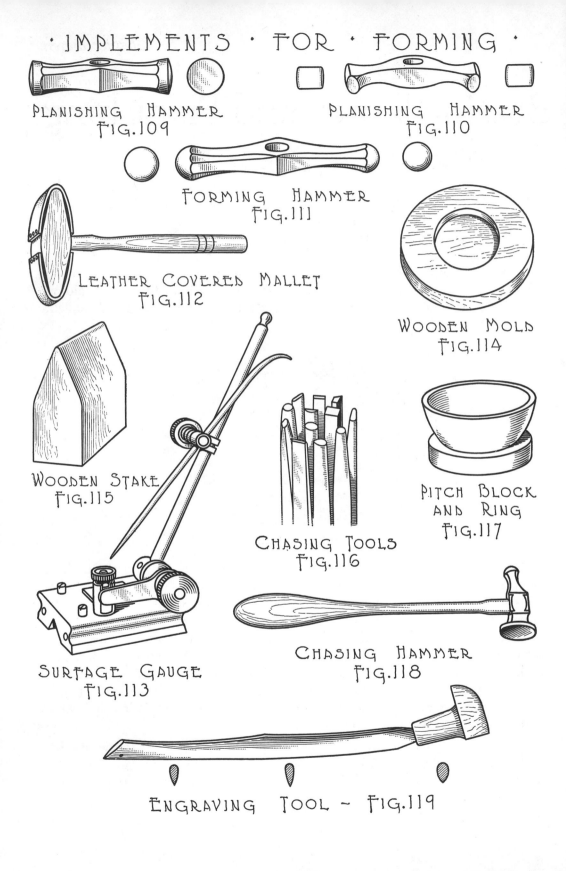

· IMPLEMENTS · FOR · FORMING ·

PLANISHING HAMMER
FIG. 109

PLANISHING HAMMER
FIG. 110

FORMING HAMMER
FIG. 111

LEATHER COVERED MALLET
FIG. 112

WOODEN MOLD
FIG. 114

WOODEN STAKE
FIG. 115

CHASING TOOLS
FIG. 116

PITCH BLOCK
AND RING
FIG. 117

SURFACE GAUGE
FIG. 113

CHASING HAMMER
FIG. 118

ENGRAVING TOOL ~ FIG. 119

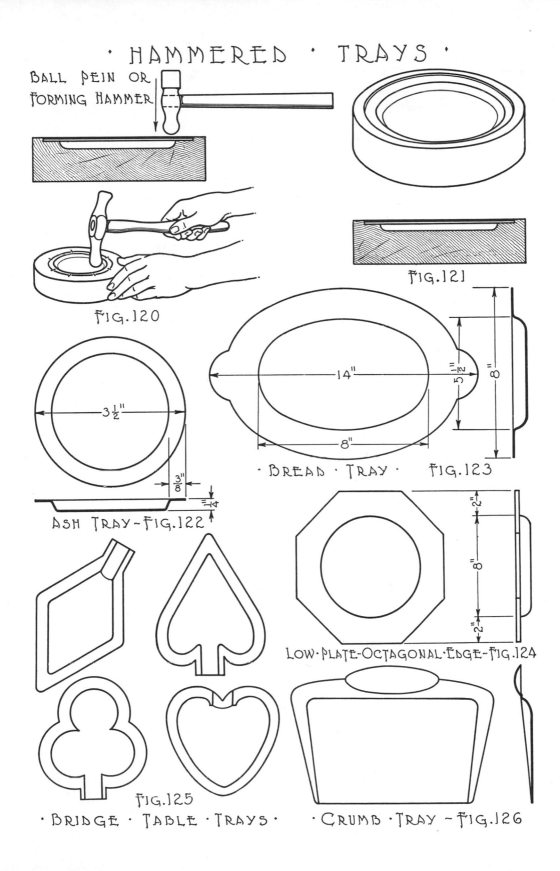

· HAMMERED · TRAYS ·

BALL PEIN OR
FORMING HAMMER

FIG.120

FIG.121

· BREAD · TRAY ·   FIG.123

14"
5 $\frac{11}{12}$
8"
8"

3 $\frac{1}{2}$"
$\frac{3}{8}$"
$\frac{1}{4}$"

ASH TRAY ~ FIG.122

LOW · PLATE · OCTAGONAL · EDGE ~ FIG.124

2"
8"
2"

· BRIDGE · TABLE · TRAYS ·   FIG.125

· CRUMB · TRAY ~ FIG.126

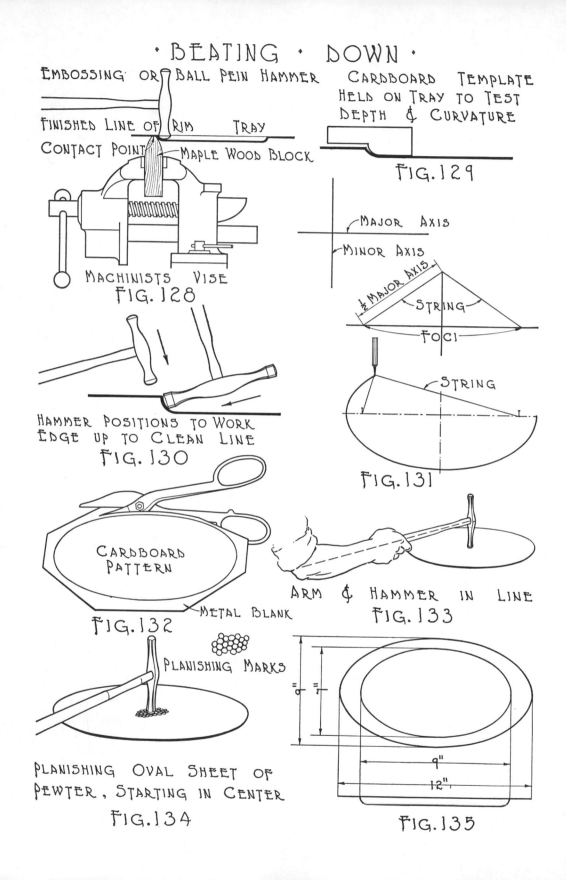

· BEATING · DOWN ·

EMBOSSING OR BALL PEIN HAMMER

FINISHED LINE OF RIM   TRAY

CONTACT POINT — MAPLE WOOD BLOCK

MACHINISTS VISE
FIG. 128

HAMMER POSITIONS TO WORK
EDGE UP TO CLEAN LINE
FIG. 130

CARDBOARD TEMPLATE
HELD ON TRAY TO TEST
DEPTH & CURVATURE
FIG. 129

MAJOR AXIS
MINOR AXIS
½ MAJOR AXIS
STRING
FOCI
STRING
FIG. 131

CARDBOARD
PATTERN
METAL BLANK
FIG. 132

ARM & HAMMER IN LINE
FIG. 133

PLANISHING MARKS

PLANISHING OVAL SHEET OF
PEWTER, STARTING IN CENTER
FIG. 134

9"
12"
FIG. 135

The top of the stake should be on a level with the worker's elbow. Hold the planishing hammer well back on the handle, keeping the arm and handle in a straight line, as in Fig. 133, with the elbow close to the side. The arm should be raised slightly and the wrist bent upward lifting the hammer one or two inches above the metal. Only slight effort is necessary to deliver a blow of sufficient weight. The hammer must strike the metal squarely so that the edge of the face will not leave a mark.

The entire area should be planished with blows that fall in such a manner that they slightly overlap. *No part of the original surface of the metal should show between the marks. The process is used to stiffen the metal, not to add useless hammer marks.*

The beating down process is carried out with the metal held over a wooden stake shaped as in Fig. 128. Hammering may be started in the center of the long side and should proceed slowly to the left. The guide line should be kept about one-eighth of an inch, or slightly more, back of the point where the metal rests on the stake.

Hold the forming hammer in the same manner as was employed for the planishing hammer. Blows should be somewhat heavier than those for planishing, but not hard enough to form bulging projections on the bottom.

Three blows are delivered in one spot, then the metal is rotated slightly in order that the next three fall to the left of the first three. This system is continued around and around until the desired depth is obtained.

As the work progresses it should be tested frequently by holding a cardboard template on the bottom and moving it up to the rim (Fig. 129).

If the tray tends to warp as it is being hammered, turn it face down on a clean smooth bench, lay a block of wood on the rim and hammer it until the tray becomes level. Occasionally this remedy is not sufficient and similar blows must be struck on the bottom, working first on the face, then on the back. Do not permit the metal to depart far from a flat plane, or it may be difficult to restore.

The rim is planished last, and a clean, fairly sharp line formed where the edge meets the curve. This line, formed by the alternate use of the planishing hammer on the rim and the forming hammer on the curve, as shown in Fig. 130, is an indication of good workmanship. The tray should now show even-sized hammer blows over the entire surface, with no conspicuous hammer marks or unhammered metal showing. Any extra metal left at the outside of the rim may now be trimmed off and the edge filed to the line.

Many articles similar to the tray may be made by forcing the metal into molds of wood or metal (Fig. 121). These molds may be purchased in a variety of shapes and sizes, or better, made by the craftsman himself. Circular molds are made on the lathe; other shapes are carved out by hand. A method of making metal molds is described in Chapter 9.

Metal hammers may be used for shaping the metal, but pewter is commonly formed by a smooth mallet of wood, horn, rawhide, or plastic composition. When the mallet is used no marks of pounding need to show on the metal.

Fig. 136—Hammered Pewter Plate

To make the small ash tray, turn a mold out of maple to the size and shape shown in Figs. 121 and 122. Cut a disc of metal four inches in diameter and place it in the mold. Proceed to direct the blows of the mallet or hammer just over the edge of the rim in the same manner as was done on the tray. This process continues until the metal reaches the bottom and fits the curve of the mold.

Remove the metal from the mold, file the edge, and polish. A small curved piece of pewter is soldered to the rim to complete the tray. The plate shown in Fig. 136, is another project involving similar methods of construction.

Chapter Eight

Raising

*T*HE COMPOTE (Figs. 137-138) is made by a process somewhat different from that used on the tray. Whereas the tray was fashioned entirely by stretching the metal below the surface of the original sheet, such forms as the compote are made by partly stretching and partly condensing the metal while raising the edge upwards. Stretching can be carried only a short distance before the metal becomes thin and somewhat weakened, but the condensing process permits raising a piece with high walls.

Fig. 137—Pewter Compote

A sand bag is an important item of equipment for this type of work (Figs. 139 and 142). It may be made of leather or canvas and may be purchased or made by the craftsman. Sand bags vary in size from 6 inches to 12 inches according to the maximum size of work to be attempted. Wooden forms of various types are required for certain problems, as shown in Fig. 143. Hammers and mallets are also necessary (see Figs. 109, 110, 111, 144 and 145). Some simple jobs of raising may be done with an ordinary ball-pein hammer, but for higher work a regular raising hammer (Fig. 140) is needed. The mallets should be of various shapes such as rounded, wedge-shaped, and flat. Templates made from stiff cardboard for testing the curves of the various projects should be prepared from full-sized drawings.

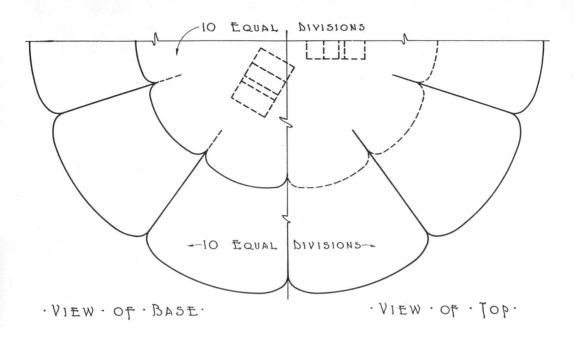

·VIEW·OF·BASE·   ·VIEW·OF·TOP·

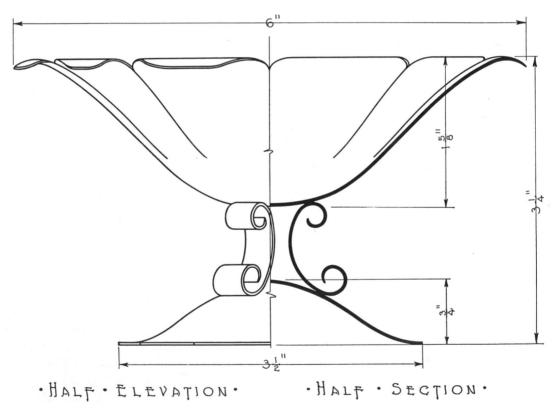

·HALF·ELEVATION·   ·HALF·SECTION·

· COMPOTE ·
FIG.138

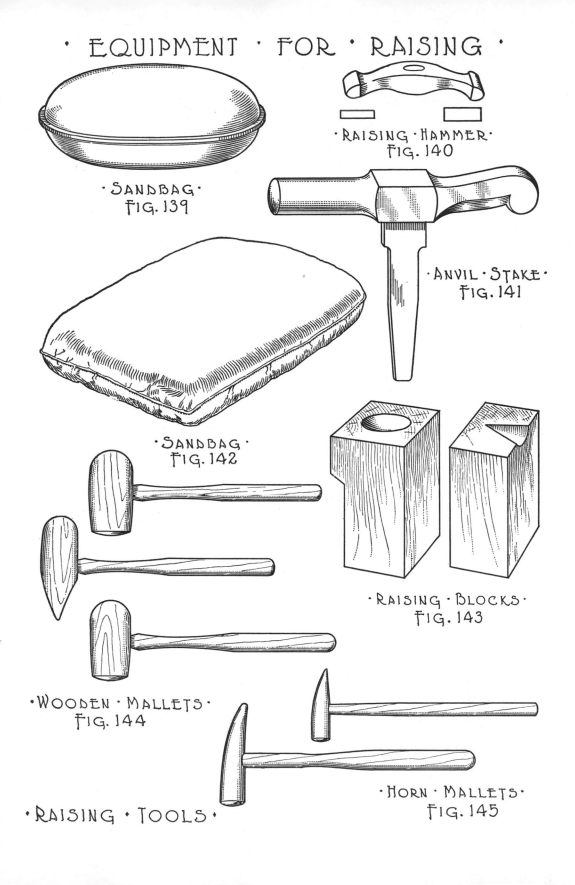

· EQUIPMENT · FOR · RAISING ·

· SANDBAG ·
FIG. 139

· RAISING · HAMMER ·
FIG. 140

· ANVIL · STAKE ·
FIG. 141

· SANDBAG ·
FIG. 142

· RAISING · BLOCKS ·
FIG. 143

· WOODEN · MALLETS ·
FIG. 144

· HORN · MALLETS ·
FIG. 145

· RAISING · TOOLS ·

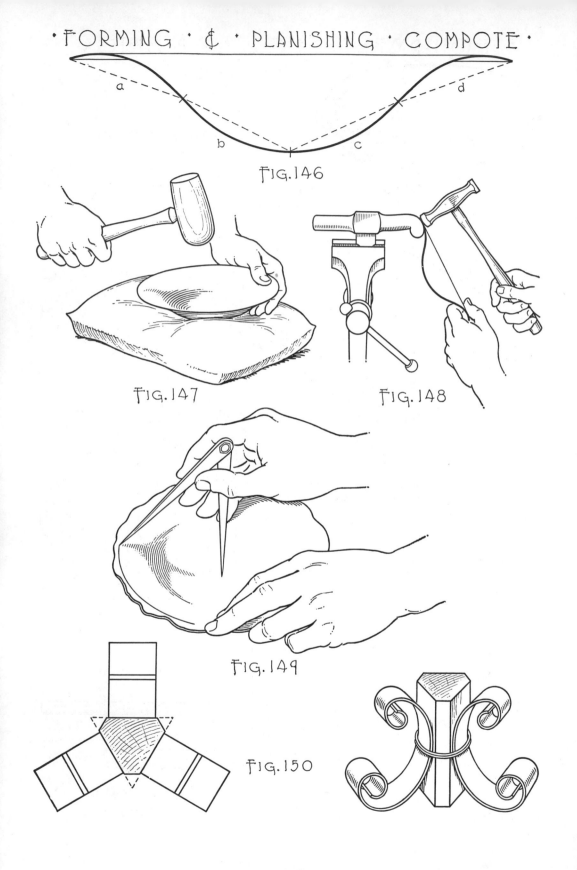

·FORMING · & · PLANISHING · COMPOTE·

FIG.146

FIG.147

FIG.148

FIG.149

FIG.150

The Compote. The amount of metal required for the compote is determined by measuring the cords subtending or describing the arcs in the outline. Hence the diameter of the blank would be the sum of the distances *a, b, c,* and *d* in Fig. 146.

The slow rather even curves of this project can be formed most conveniently on the sand bag. Place the disc over the center and start beating down with a rounded mallet as in Fig. 147. The blows need not be heavy as the metal moves rather easily under the strokes. The triple stroke described in Chapter 7 should be used here. As the work begins to assume shape it should be tested frequently with the template and the hammer blows shifted as requisite. When the form coincides with the template, the metal should be placed upon a metal or hardwood anvil stake (Fig. 141) as shown in Fig. 148, and planished on the outside with a smooth, flat hammer. The stake should fit the curvature of the metal exactly or the shape of the compote will be spoiled.

Fig. 151—Hammered Sugar and Creamer

When the complete surface has been planished, the outer edge should be marked for trimming by placing a pair of dividers with one point at the center and the other near the outer edge as shown in Fig. 149. Mark the circle by revolving the dish. Then, holding the metal in the left hand and the snips as shown in Fig. 132, trim to the line. Chapter 9 should be consulted at this point concerning the method of completing the bowl by fluting. The disc for the base should be prepared and worked up in exactly the same manner except that it is not fluted.

The length of the connecting supports may be determined by sketching full size and bending a narrow strip of sheet metal or wire to conform with the curve. This gauge may then be straightened and the measurement determined. Cut and file the edges to exact size and form the strips over a round rod starting at each end and working toward the center. A soft mallet should be

CREAM · PITCHER ·

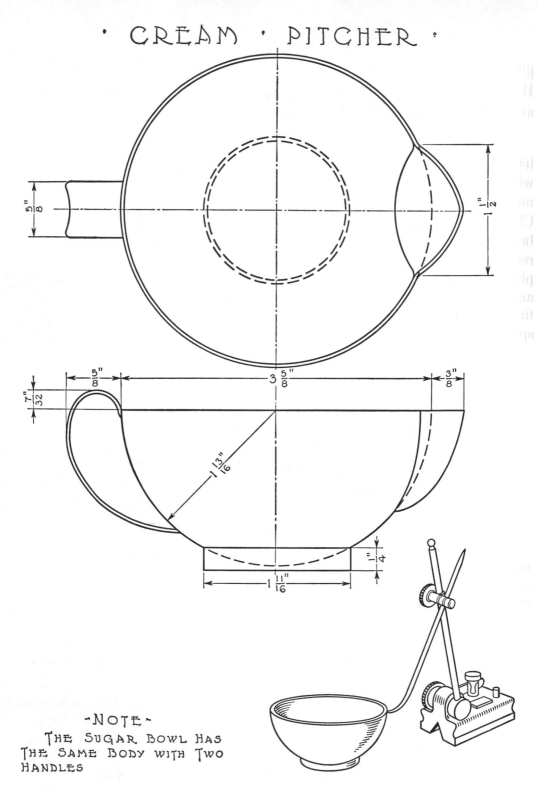

$\frac{5}{8}''$

$1\frac{1}{2}''$

$\frac{5}{8}''$ $3\frac{5}{8}''$ $\frac{3}{8}''$

$\frac{7}{32}''$

$1\frac{13}{16}''$

$\frac{1}{4}''$

$1\frac{11}{16}''$

-NOTE-
THE SUGAR BOWL HAS
THE SAME BODY WITH TWO
HANDLES

FIG.152

· RAISING · ON · STAKE ·

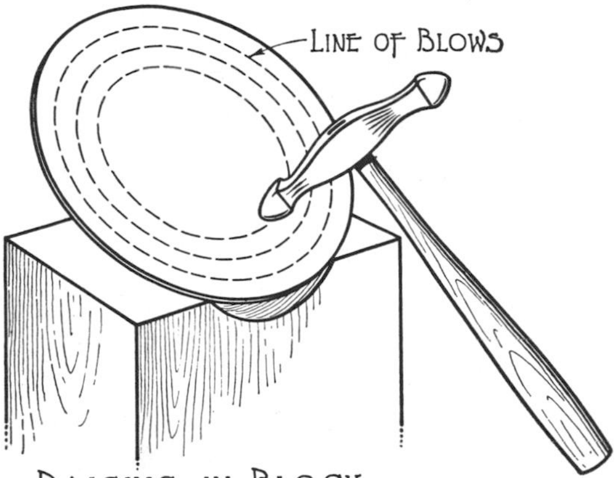

Line of Blows

**RAISING IN BLOCK
FIG. 153**

FIG. 154

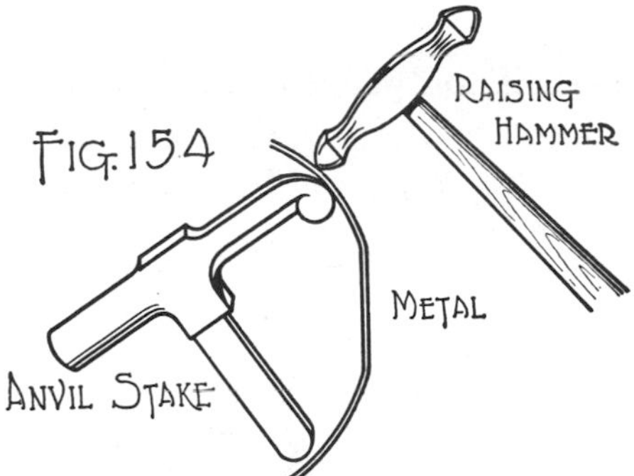

RAISING HAMMER

METAL

ANVIL STAKE

THE HAMMER STRIKES ABOUT $\frac{1}{8}''$ ABOVE
THE POINT WHERE THE METAL RESTS
ON THE STAKE.
RAISING A BOWL ON A STAKE

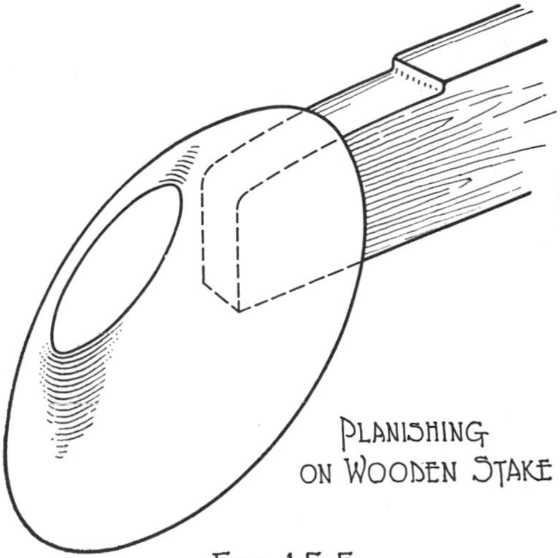

PLANISHING
ON WOODEN STAKE
FIG. 155

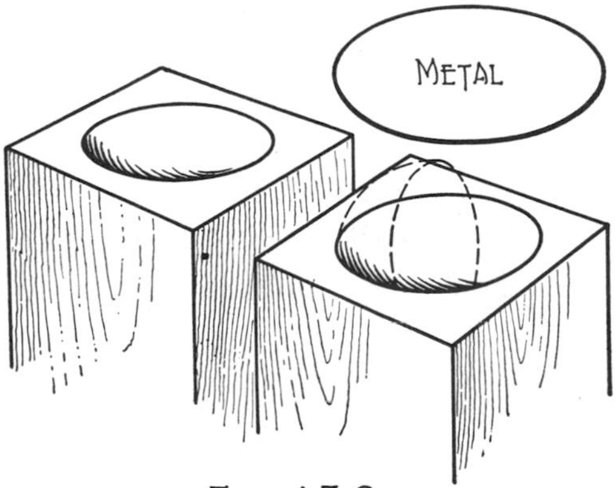

METAL

FIG. 156

**PORRINGER
FIG. 157**

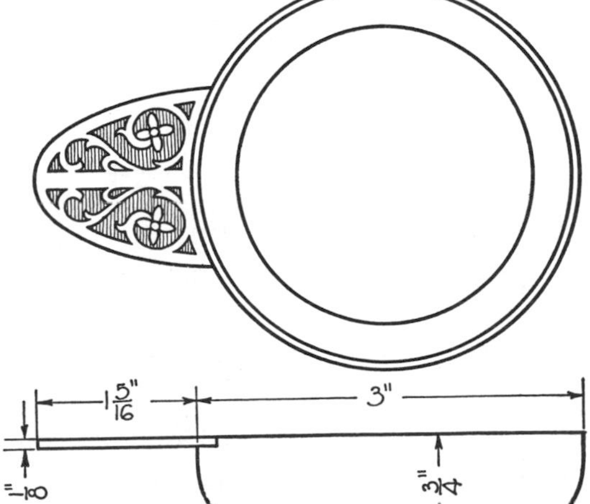

$1\frac{5}{16}''$

$3''$

$\frac{1}{16}''$

$\frac{3}{4}''$

FIG. 158

used if the metal cannot be bent with the fingers. All parts of the compote should be thoroughly polished, however, before the links are attached.

Soldering the links requires the use of a simple jig to hold the pieces in place while the heat is being applied. Cut a three-cornered piece of wood about 2 inches long with each face about ¼ of an inch longer than the width of the strips. Place the links against the faces and wire them together as shown in Fig. 150. Set them upon the base and adjust until they are even and centered. Apply a flux to all three joints and solder by the direct method after which the wooden piece should be removed, but the binding wire retained. Invert the compote on the table; place the base with the links attached in its correct position, and solder. Use 63-37 solder for all joints. Clean away the excess solder as described in Chapter 4 and give a final polish.

Sugar and Creamer. A somewhat different form of raising is involved in making the sugar and creamer shown in Fig. 151. Curves of this character may best be executed in a wooden form as shown in Fig. 143. These stakes are made from some hard, close-grained wood such as maple, birch, or dogwood, the groove being formed with a gouge or wood rasp. This groove must be changed as the work progresses to keep the contour of the dish as desired. It should be rather shallow when starting and gradually made deeper.

The blank is held at an angle of 25 to 30 degrees over the groove of the block, as shown in Fig. 153. The first hammer blows are struck about two inches from the edge, and as the work is revolved the hammering proceeds outward. When the edge is reached the groove may be slightly deepened and the process repeated, beginning slightly closer to the center. Test with the template frequently and continue hammering until the desired shape is attained.

The sugar and creamer may be planished over metal stakes if they are available, or a hardwood stake may be formed to fit the inside curvature as shown in Fig. 155.

When thoroughly planished the top edges should be marked and trimmed in a manner similar to that described for the compote. Forming the spout is the final process in shaping. A groove of the shape required is filed in the edge of a hardwood block. With the side of the cream pitcher against the block, the metal is beaten into the groove with a raising hammer or a wedge-shaped mallet.

Determine the length of the handle from the full-sized sketch and cut from metal not thinner than 16-gauge. It should be slightly dished toward the inside to add strength and stiffness. Bend into shape and after fitting to match the curve at the top and bottom, fasten in place with iron binding wire. Solder as described in Chapter 5 using 63-37 solder. Cut and shape the ring for the base and wire together. The cream pitcher should be filled with sand, a board placed over the top, and then inverted. Locate the ring carefully and solder. The sugar bowl should be treated in the same manner. Remove all excess solder and polish with steel-wool, tripoli, and rouge.

Raising on a Stake. Cylindrical bowls, vases, or similar articles may be raised by hammering over a wooden or a polished steel anvil stake. A line is scribed on the disc of metal to define the base, and the metal is planished in this area. The disc is held in such a manner that the scribed line rests on the

Fig. 159—Beaten Porringer

surface of the stake and triple blows struck about one-eighth of an inch above the line, forcing the metal to the stake. The disc is rotated and three more blows struck at the left of the first marks, overlapping them slightly (Fig. 154). This process is continued around the metal, after which it will be noted that the diameter of the disc has been reduced under the blows. The metal is shifted back so that the hammer marks rest on the stake, and a new ring of blows is laid directly above and touching the first one. This method is continued to the rim of the piece, then repeated, starting at or close to the base. A template should be made from the working drawing and continuously used to test progress. As soon as the lower portion has reached the right shape, hammering on that part is discontinued, and concentrated on the upper portion until it, too, conforms to the pattern.

FIG. 160

FIG. 161

FIG. 162

FIG. 163

FIG. 164

FIG. 165

FIG. 166

FIG. 167

FIG. 168

Porringers. A fourth type of raising is used in making the porringer shown in Figs. 157-8-9. A circular depression is formed in the end grain of hard wood by turning in the lathe, by hand-cutting with a gouge, or by simply hammering a hole into a heavy block. The disc is first placed over the depression as shown in Fig. 156, and beaten into it as deeply as possible. It is then raised at an angle to the block and the edge beaten up until the desired height is reached. In attaining this end it is sometimes necessary to use forms of progressive depths.

After the raising is completed, the surface should be planished as already described. The bottom should be made flat by hammering with a mallet over a flat stake or block of wood. Work first from the inside of the dish and then from the outside until the metal is flat. In marking the edge for trimming, the porringer should be placed upon a flat surface; the surface gauge adjusted to the correct height and moved around the metal leaving a light line on it. If no surface gauge is available, a scriber or pencil may be held at the correct height on a block of wood.

As explained in Chapter 3, the design of any particular article may be considered from the historical or the functional approach. Either concept may be used in the development of the porringer handle. Considered from the historical viewpoint one has a number of excellent examples which may be copied. Some of these are English in their origin while others are distinctly American. Figs. 166 and 167 show two of the former, while the design of Fig. 168 is definitely American, from a porringer by John Danforth. Fig. 165 pictures a notable pattern after a silver porringer by Paul Revere.

Functionally, the handle must be strong and large enough to lift the weight of the dish and its contents. Within these limitations the designer may give free rein to his artistic tendencies. Figs. 161, 162, and 164 show several types which strike a modern note, while the possibilities of using initials as a basis of handle design is illustrated by Figs. 160 and 163.

It is necessary that the metal forming the handle be heavy enough to safeguard against bending with continued use. To provide this strength the part is usually cast. (It may be cut from 12- or 14-gauge sheet pewter). After the design has been decided upon and drawn full size, it should be traced on thin paper. Using a piece of glass as a base, roll out a piece of plasticene, modeling wax, or "ozokerite," to the thickness wanted. Lay the tracing paper on the wax, and prick through it with a needle, making points about one-eighth of an inch apart, and at all ends of lines. Remove the paper and with a sharp knife cut away the portions which form the open parts of the handle. In performing this operation, care should be taken to hold the knife

· ATTACHING · PORRINGER · HANDLE ·

FIG. 169

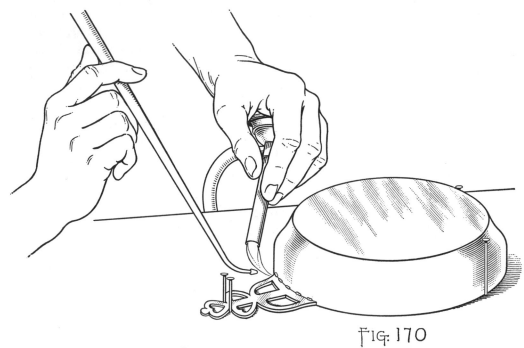

FIG. 170

FIG. 171

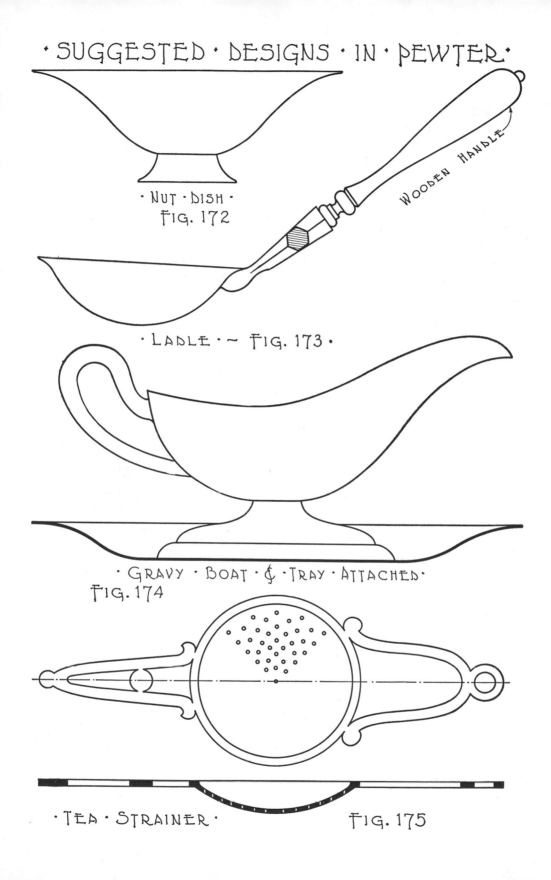

· SUGGESTED · DESIGNS · IN · PEWTER ·

· NUT · DISH ·
FIG. 172

WOODEN HANDLE

· LADLE · ~ FIG. 173 ·

· GRAVY · BOAT · & · TRAY · ATTACHED ·
FIG. 174

· TEA · STRAINER ·   FIG. 175

at a slight angle to make the bottom of the opening slightly smaller than the top. This precaution provides for "draft," which allows the casting to be drawn from the mold. The surface of the wax may be smoothed and the corners rounded by rubbing with the finger-tip, moistened with glycerine.

When the model is complete build a form around it as described in Chapter 6, and cover with plaster of Paris. Give sufficient time for the mold to set, detach it from the glass, and remove the wax pattern. The plaster should then be thoroughly dried. Cut a pouring gate at the point where the handle joins the rim, make any necessary vents, and smoke the inside surface of the mold. A plain piece of plaster cast upon a glass or a piece of wood should be placed against the mold, the two tied firmly together, and the metal poured.

When cool, remove the casting, cut off the gate, and file out any imperfections or irregularities with jeweler's files. Fit the joint carefully where the handle is fastened to the bowl. This fit may be made by laying the bowl beside the handle and marking the curvature with a pair of dividers, as illustrated in Fig. 171. Be sure to put pencil marks on the edge of the bowl, so that in filing the trials will be made against the same part of the rim each time. When a satisfactory fit is secured, place the handle and bowl upside down upon an asbestos pad, and fasten it in position as shown in Fig. 169. Apply the flux and snippets of 63-37 solder, and sweat the joint together by the direct method (Fig. 170). Intricate parts of the design may be cleaned up with narrow strips of emery cloth, and a final polish given to the whole porringer with tripoli and rouge.

Fig. 176—Tea Strainer

By similar processes many other useful and artistic articles of pewter ware may be fashioned, the nut dish, Fig. 172, the ladle, Fig. 173, the gravy boat and tray, Fig. 174, and the tea strainer, Figs. 175 and 176, being offered as suggestions to the student of the pewter craft.

Chapter Nine

Decorative Processes

*T*HE CRAFTSMAN may find it desirable to increase or decrease the amount of emphasis given to certain lines, areas, or volumes in his product. Qualities that attract interest may be enhanced by introducing lines different in character from those of the remainder of the article. An effect of lightness and of satisfying completion may be secured by means of breaking up strong solid lines by sawing and filing the outline to the shape desired.

Sawing. A support should be made for sawing like that shown in Fig. 42. A jeweler's saw frame is shown in Fig. 40. Blades with various size teeth may be used, but those numbered 1, 2, 3, and 4 are most suitable for pewter. Care should be taken that the metal does not move and that the part near the blade rests solidly on the support at all times. The saw is usually held with the blade as nearly vertical as possible, and is moved up and down, cutting on the down stroke. Only slight forward pressure is required to cut the metal. Too much pressure, from haste, or turning the metal while the saw is at rest, often results in snapping the blade. When such an accident occurs, the larger pieces may be used by shortening the saw frame.

Reeding. Strength can be given to an edge by means of a plain reed soldered to the tray as shown in Fig. 177, or by means of the rolled edge as in Fig. 178. An example of a more elaborate or decorative reeding is illustrated in Fig. 180 (trophy cup). This type of reeding may be purchased if desired. Simply cut a strip of paper the width of the reed and wrap it around the article in position. Cut this paper to correct length and use it as a pattern for cutting the reed. Curves that cannot be fitted with paper may be measured or stepped off by dividers with the points set about one-half inch apart.

Cut the strip of reeding slightly over length, fit it to the article by bending with the fingers, file the ends to an exact fit, and hold in place with clips (Fig. 179). Flux the metal, apply snippets of solder, and play a flame along the reed, heating as uniformly as possible until the solder melts and runs through the joint. The decorative effect of reading is well illustrated in the trophy cup pictured in Fig. 181.

Area Enrichment. One of the most effective methods of enriching the surface of pewter is by taking advantage of its texture and color and to leaving large smooth areas, or by planishing the surface.

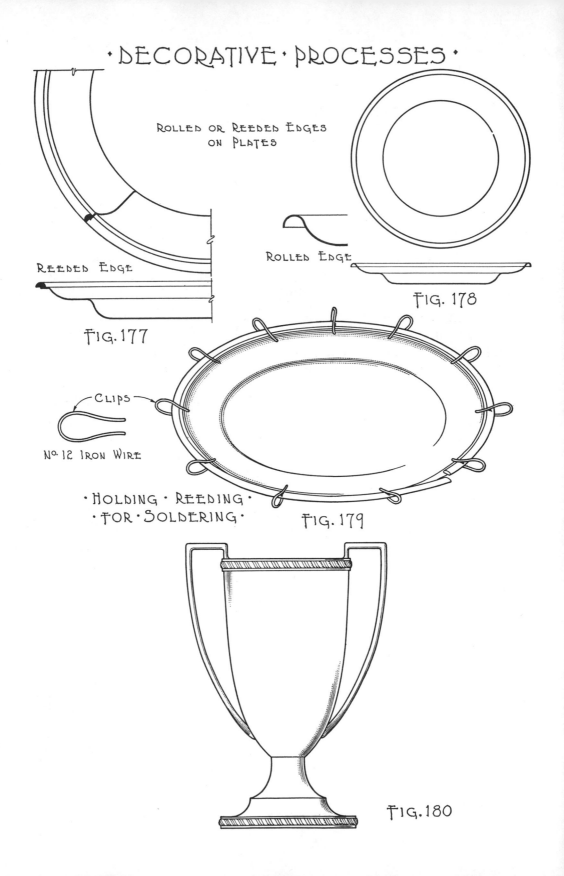

· DECORATIVE · PROCESSES ·

ROLLED OR REEDED EDGES
ON PLATES

REEDED EDGE

FIG. 177

ROLLED EDGE

FIG. 178

CLIPS

Nº 12 IRON WIRE

· HOLDING · REEDING ·
· FOR · SOLDERING ·

FIG. 179

FIG. 180

Applique. If large surfaces are not desired, parts may be divided artistically, or small areas of attractive interest can be developed, through building up levels by soldering on one or more layers of metal. When pewter is used, this added metal must seem to grow naturally from the surface. Contrasting metals, such as copper, stand out very distinctly against the soft-colored background. These applique decorations should have a contour paralleling that of the surface on which they are placed, or be so shaped that their outlines harmonize with the surrounding contour.

Before cutting the metal for the applique, prepare a paper pattern and fit it in place to gauge its suitability. Paste this pattern on a piece of metal and cut to shape with snips or saw. File to the finish line and polish. If any enrichment is to be a part of this applique, it should be developed before any soldering is done. For example, the match box (Figs. 182 and 183) is shown with a pewter applique upon which a few straight lines are engraved.

The back of this piece should then be "tinned" by cleaning, applying flux and solder, and heating until the solder flows over the surface to within about one-eighth of an inch of the edge. The area on which the applique is to be placed

Fig. 181—Trophy Cup

should also be tinned, again stopping short of the outline of the pattern.

Next apply flux, hold the pieces together with clips, and apply heat evenly until the solder melts. This condition can be detected sometimes by a slight movement or settling of the applique. Leave the clips in place until the metal cools enough to permit handling. This delay will insure sufficient time for the solder to harden.

If any solder has flowed from under the edge, it may be removed with an engraving tool or a small piece of fine emery cloth. Then the usual cleaning and polishing can proceed.

Fluting. Strength can be given to some articles by fluting certain areas. Fluting is a type of surface enrichment that adds to the structural quality as well as the interest of the piece on which it is placed. The fluting may be made up of similar size spacing, or of symmetrical arrangements of various size spaces.

· DECORATIVE · PROCESSES ·
· MATCH · BOX · COVER ·

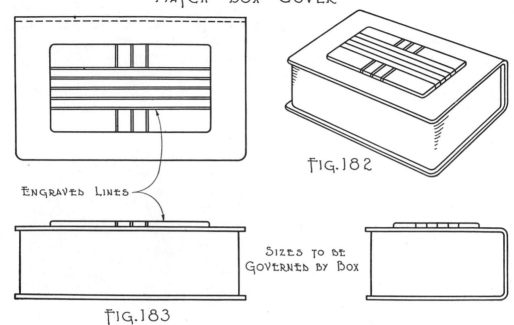

ENGRAVED LINES

FIG.182

SIZES TO BE
GOVERNED BY BOX

FIG.183

· ORNAMENTAL · INSET ·

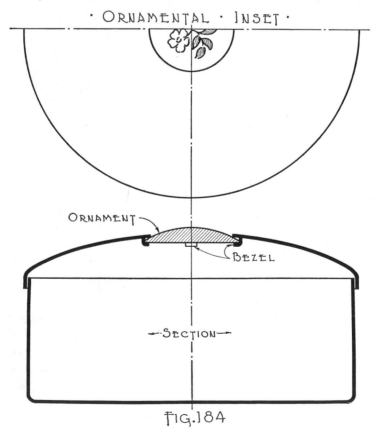

ORNAMENT

BEZEL

←SECTION→

FIG.184

Turn or shape a maple block to fit the curvature of the outside of the compote (Fig. 186). Gouge a groove in this block from the rim to a point about one inch from the bottom, gradually decreasing the depth until it tapers out to the surface of the block. Divide the rim of the compote into divisions of the proper number and size and run light guide lines from the rim to the center of the bottom to define the center of each groove.

Set the bowl on the block in such a position that the guide line coincides with the center of the groove in the block. Force the metal into the block with a wooden mallet until it fits the bottom (Fig. 186). Lay out the line for the rim, saw out, and file to a smooth edge.

Chasing and Embossing. Outlines or surfaces may be given emphasis by chasing and embossing. The contour may be paralleled by a chased line, or by a sequence of slightly raised decorative elements. This work is done with the metal held over a block of lead or placed on a pitch block.

The plate for the candle sconce (Figs. 189 and 315) should be cut out, leaving one-fourth of an inch margin of extra metal all around the edge (Fig. 187). Lay out guide lines on the surface to indicate the outline of each embossed area. Oil the metal slightly on the back and lay it on a pitch pan. Warm the metal a little by playing a small flame around over the surface until the pitch takes hold. Set a straight chasing tool, or tracer, on one of the straight lines and strike with the hammer. Repeat the process to the end of the line, using great care to have the tool marks continuous and indented to the same depth (Fig. 187). Select a curved tool to conform to the curvature of the rounded parts, and chase them in the same manner. The rim should be outlined with a tool having a very slight curvature.

Carefully warm the metal again and lift from the pitch. Clean the pitch from the under side and replace on the pitch pan, this time face downward. It will be noted that the traced outline appears as a raised line on this side. At this point it would be well to lay a scrap piece of pewter on the pitch, and practise using the rounded chasing tools to produce a smooth, even surface on an embossed area (Fig. 188).

When skill and confidence are gained, proceed to emboss the sconce. A template of thin hard cardboard will help to secure a uniform depth, if used constantly (Fig. 188). A second template can be used to gauge the taper in depth from the outer to the inner end.

Emboss the groove around the rim and the circle in the center. Warm the metal again, remove it from the pitch, and clean. It may be necessary to

~FLUTING ~ CHASING ~ EMBOSSING ~

FIG. 185

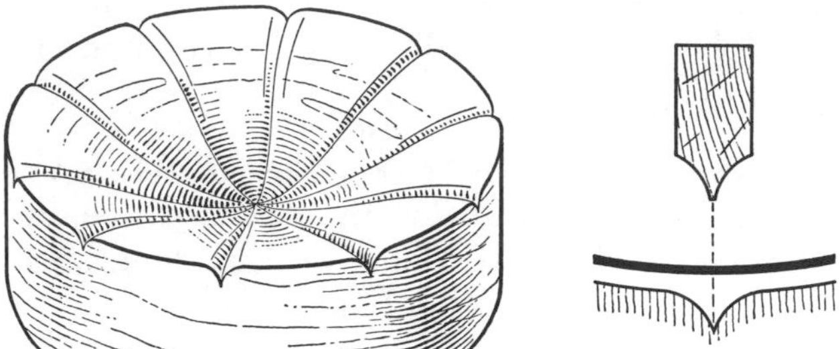

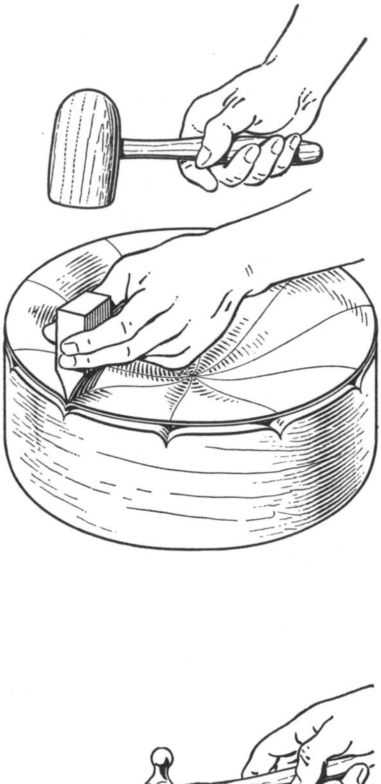

FIG. 186

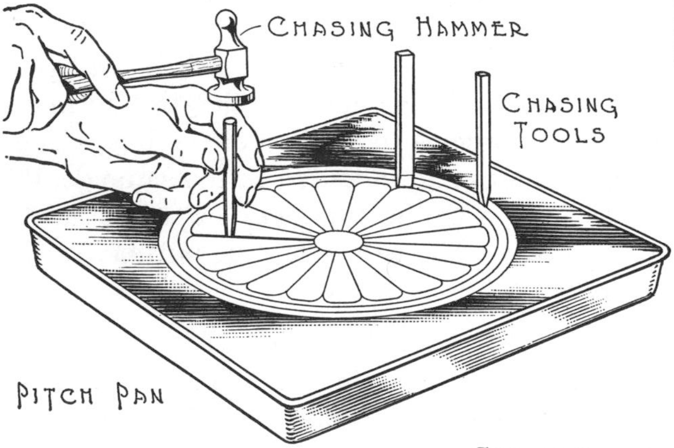

CHASING HAMMER

CHASING
TOOLS

PITCH PAN

FIG. 187

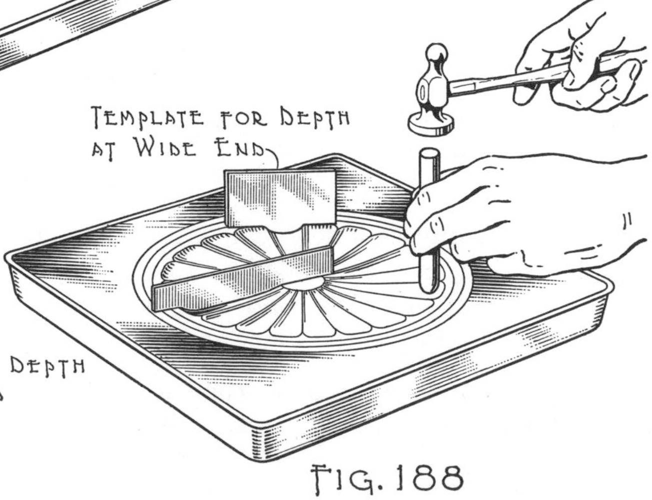

TEMPLATE FOR DEPTH
AT WIDE END

TEMPLATE FOR DEPTH
AT BOTTOM

FIG. 188

repeat the chasing and embossing on both sides several times. Trim and file away the extra metal around the rim and test for flatness by laying the piece on a level surface.

The candle socket may be made by the same process that was used for the ink bottle holder. The tray may be beaten down in a mold similar to that used for the porringer.

Fourteen-gauge pewter should be used for the bracket. This metal is shaped over a wooden stake and planished to give stiffness. Solder the parts and clean as previously described.

Ornamental Inset. A device for adding interest to some spot or appendage is that of setting in a decorative piece of copper or other metal, a stone, plastic, or ceramic ornament.

The texture and color of pewter make many articles unsuited for this purpose. Bright colors must be used sparingly, while greyed tones can be used over larger areas. Highly carved stones do not match the soft finish of the metal as well as do those of low relief.

Fig. 189—Candle Sconce, Chased and Embossed

A jewel box is shown with a ceramic plaque inserted in the top (Fig. 184). No sizes are given, since these must vary with the ornament selected. This article may be built up by the same process as that used in Chapter 4, or it may be spun. A circle, slightly smaller than the plaque is marked on the top, and the metal cut out. A bezel is formed to fit around the plaque and soldered to the metal on the under side. After the ornament is in place, the edge of the bezel is burnished with a smooth piece of steel to bend it over the ornament.

Piercing and Sawing. Another device for adding attractiveness to small areas is that of piercing the metal with a pattern. The porringer handles described in Chapter 8 could, if desired, be made by sawing out the designs with a jeweler's saw from 12-gauge metal. Since piercing weakens the handle, metal of sufficient thickness must be used to overcome this fault, and the cut-out portions placed to retain maximum strength.

Etching. Patterns may be produced on the surface by etching, although this art is probably one of the least desirable forms of decoration for pewter.

Designs for etching should be rather broad in character, avoiding delicate details.

An etched pattern may be put on the bottom of the coaster (Fig. 267) as follows: Clean the metal thoroughly, and avoid touching the parts that are to be etched. Any oil coming in contact with the metal will weaken the acid-resisting ground.

To transfer the pattern to the metal, paint the surface with any light tempera color. Lay the drawing of the design over a piece of carbon paper on the tempera and outline the pattern with a sharp pencil. Remove the paper and lightly scratch the outline into the pewter with a stylus.

Wash off the tempera and dry the metal with a soft cloth. Paint on a liquid form of etcher's ground (or liquid asphaltum) with a small soft brush, and permit it to dry thoroughly. If the article is small it should be entirely covered with the ground, except for the design; if large, the ground should be applied for about an inch around the outside of the pattern.

(Courtesy of the Metropolitan Museum of Art)

**Fig. 190—Two-Handled Bowl and Cover (probably French),
18th Century**

Pour enough nitric acid into a glass container of water, to make about a twenty-per cent solution. *Do not make the mistake of pouring water into the acid, or an explosion may take place.* Immerse the metal in the acid solution and observe the bubbles. These indicate that the acid is attacking the metal. This process should be performed under a hood or out-of-doors, or where there is a current of air to carry off the fumes. Continue the etching until the metal is removed to a depth of about one thirty-second of an inch. The depth may be gauged by occasionally lifting the piece from the acid, washing it in clear water, and examining it in a strong light. If asphaltum is used, then the surface must be watched carefully throughout the entire process, as it has a tendency to break loose from the metal.

If etching is done on an article of any considerable size, a wall of modeling wax or beeswax should be built up around the pattern and the acid poured into this space. When the desired depth is reached, pour off the acid, wash and dry the piece, then remove the ground with benzene or gasoline.

Engraving. Engraving is an important process of decoration on old pewter, but is used very sparingly today. A common historic device is the "joggled" or "wriggled" line, which is well illustrated in the 18th century French piece shown in Fig. 190. This decoration was produced by means of a narrow chisel which was simply rocked from end to end of the cutting edge, then turned to the next position and repeated.

(Courtesy of the Johnson-Humerickhouse Memorial Museum, Coshocton, Ohio)

Fig. 191—Engraved Pewter Plate, 17th Century

Engraving tools (Fig. 119) may be used to cut a pattern of lines in the metal. Fig. 191 shows a 17th-century piece of pewter subjected to this process. When using engraving tools, the metal should be held firmly or attached to a pitch bowl. This bowl may be set on a sand bag to facilitate turning (see Fig. 185). The left hand must not be put in front of the tool, since a slip (which frequently happens to the beginner) may result in a bad cut.

Engraved lines which follow the circumference of cylindrical articles may be made on the lathe. The metal must run very accurately, or the line will be deep on one side and taper off entirely on the other. This method of decoration is an effective means of emphasizing contour. It may also serve to trace a soldered joint (Fig. 300).

Chapter Ten

Casting

A DOOR KNOCKER is an article rarely executed in pewter. The addition of brass or bronze inserts to the colonial type shown in Fig. 192 to furnish the knocking points, makes of it an object of utility as well as distinctive appearance.

The Back Plate. A full-size drawing should be prepared for the wood pattern of the back plate. Cut two pieces of mahogany or soft pine and finish them to ½ in. by 3 in. by 7½ in. as shown in Fig. 194. (Mahogany is best suited for this type of pattern.) Glue the pieces together with a strong paper between as described in Chapter 6. When the glue is thoroughly dry, lay out centers on each end. Draw a center line along one face, and paste a full-size tracing of the outline upon the block, centering it on the line mentioned above. Cut along the outside of the line with a jig- or coping-saw, leaving sufficient stock at the ends so that the lathe centers will hold solidly. Both ends of the pattern may now be turned as far as the points *A-A* and *B-B* (see Fig. 193). Separate the paper which holds the pattern together, and select the better section for finishing.

Fig. 192—Colonial Door Knocker

The part of the pattern between *A-A* and *B-B* must be shaped by hand. This operation may be performed entirely with a knife, file, and sandpaper; or pattern maker's chisels and carving tools may be employed. A small belt sander may be used effectively in thinning the center part of the plate. Finally, a thorough sanding with fine sandpaper should remove all rough spots and leave a perfectly smooth surface.

Clapper. A full-size drawing of the clapper should be laid out on a piece of wood one-half inch thick and sawed to the outline with a jig- or coping-saw. Thin the portions away from the center as indicated in Fig. 193 with a knife, chisel, or file. Work the terminals into shape, being careful not to break the pins which act as hinges. Shape the diamond at the center of the clapper, and thoroughly sand all surfaces. At this point both parts of the pattern should

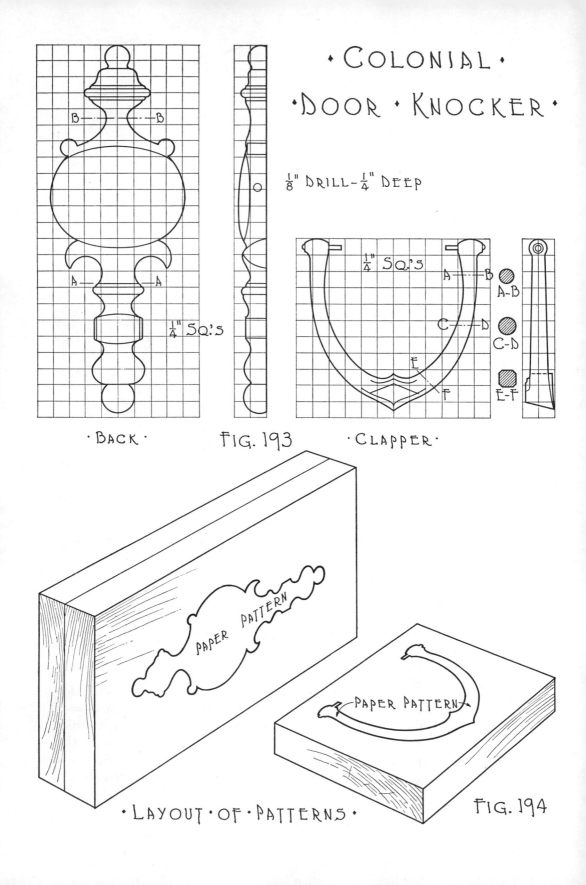

· COLONIAL ·
· DOOR · KNOCKER ·

$\frac{1}{8}$" DRILL – $\frac{1}{4}$" DEEP

B — — B

A — — A

$\frac{1}{4}$" SQ.'S

· BACK ·

FIG. 193

$\frac{1}{4}$" SQ.'S

A — — B

A-B

C — — D

C-D

E

F

E-F

· CLAPPER ·

PAPER PATTERN

PAPER PATTERN

· LAYOUT · OF · PATTERNS ·

FIG. 194

· EQUIPMENT · FOR · CASTING ·

LIFTING SCREW FOR
METAL PATTERN
FIG. 195

HEART & OVAL SPOON
FIG. 196

SLICK & OVAL SPOON
FIG. 197

FINISHING TROWEL
FIG. 198

SPRUE HOLE CUTTER
FIG. 199

BELLOWS
FIG. 202

PARTING COMPOUND
IN COTTON SACK
FIG. 200

BULB SPONGE
FIG. 201

RIDDLE
FIG. 203

HAND RAMMER
FOR BENCH WORK
FIG. 205

GATE CUTTER
FIG. 204

SNAP FLASK
FIG. 206

BOTTOM BOARD
FIG. 207

be carefully examined to make sure that there is sufficient "draft" (taper) to the sides for them to be removed easily from the mold. They should then be given at least two coats of shellac, rubbing between coats with fine (No. 00) steel wool.

Molding and Casting. The door knocker lends itself particularly well to casting in sand and will be used to exemplify this technique. It might, however, be made from plaster casts as explained in Chapter 6. The equipment needed may be noted in Figs. 195 to 207. The sand should be very fine, the grade commonly known as brass sand or No. 00 Albany being most suitable. The first step is the preparation of the sand. This preparation is technically known as tempering (see Fig. 208). Water is added and thoroughly mixed in until the sand forms a firm ball when grasped in the hand. The impression of the fingers should show clearly and the lump should break, leaving sharp, distinct coners. The greatest care should be taken not to add too much water. If the sand is too wet, faulty castings are sure to result, and there is the added danger that steam will form in the mold and throw the metal out with sufficient force to burn the person doing the pouring.

When the sand is properly tempered lay the patterns on a flat surface (molding board) as shown in Fig. 209. The drag or bottom part of the molding

Fig. 208—Testing Molding Sand for Temper

flask is now laid *bottom side up* over the patterns (see Fig. 210). Riddle or sift enough of the tempered molding sand over the patterns to cover all parts to a depth of at least half an inch, and pack firmly around the pattern with the fingers (Fig. 211). The surface of the sand should then be roughened by cutting with a slick (Fig. 197). Finish filling the drag with unriddled sand, and pack down firmly with a rammer (Figs. 205 and 212). If more sand is needed after ramming, the packed surface should be roughened so that the new sand will adhere. Continue filling and ramming the drag until it is full and then strike off excess sand with a straight board or bar. Next, place another board over the top of the drag and turn right side up, being sure to lift the bottom board at the same time so the patterns will not be disturbed.

Smooth the sand carefully around the back plate, then with a slick or any thin knife-like tool cut the sand down to the largest part (parting line)

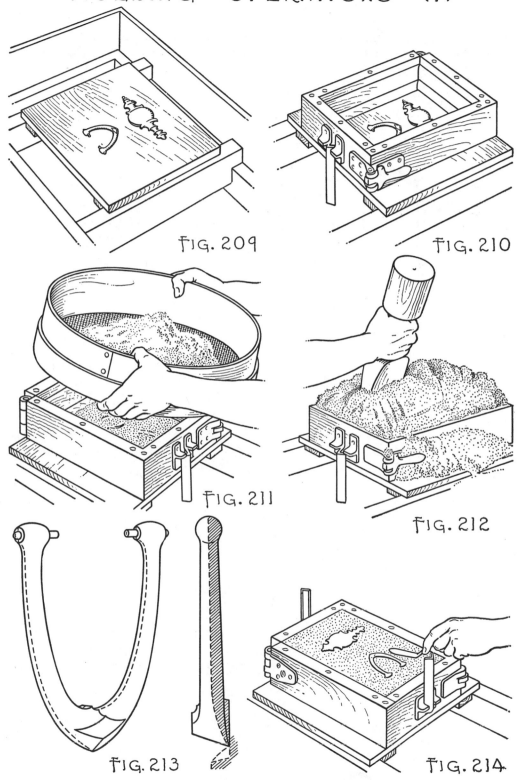

FIG. 209

FIG. 210

FIG. 211

FIG. 212

FIG. 213

FIG. 214

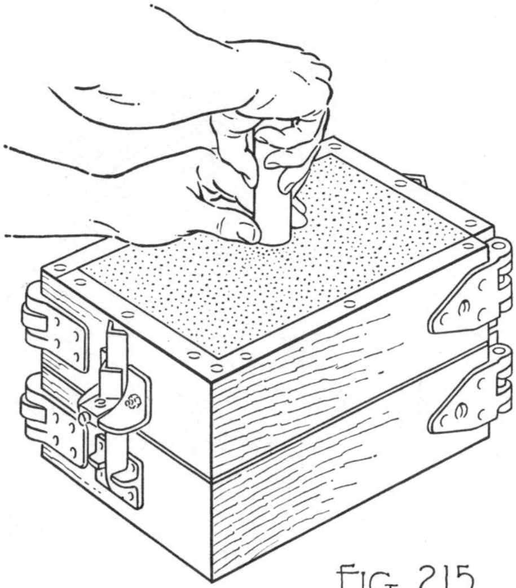

FIG. 215

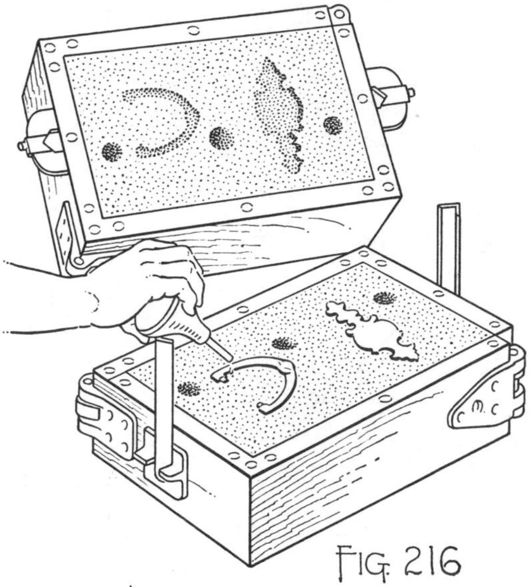

FIG. 216

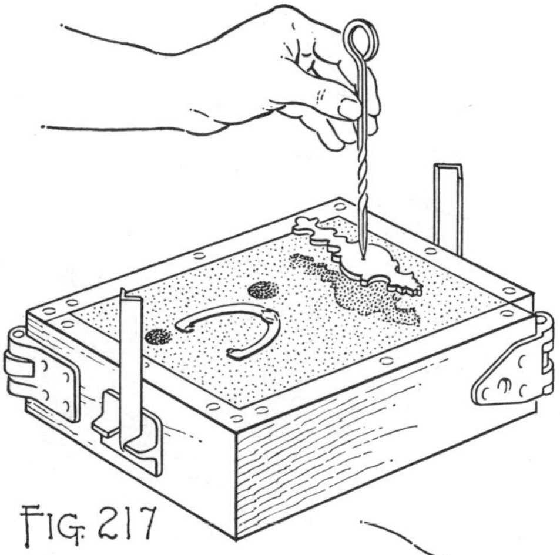

FIG. 217

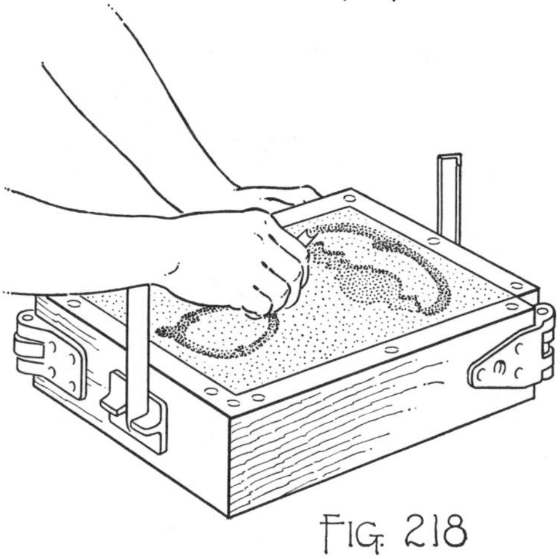

FIG. 218

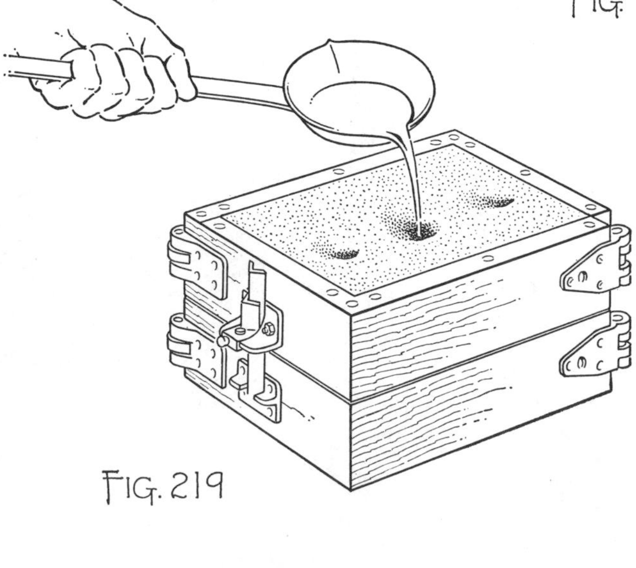

FIG. 219

of the clapper (see dotted line in Figs. 213 and 214). The sand should be slanted back from the parting line to give a gradual slope, as too sharp an angle may cause the sand to stick around the pattern. Cover the surface of the sand with some kind of *parting compound* (Fig. 200). Ordinary dry sharp sand may be used or the regular molders' parting compound may be secured at any foundry.

Next, place the cope or top part of the flask in place upon the drag, noting carefully the relative positions of the two patterns, and riddle (see Fig. 203) in sufficient sand to completely cover them. Finish filling the cope with sand, and using the wedge end of the rammer, pack the sand toward the outside of the cope. Add more sand if necessary and pack solidly until the cope is filled.

The sprue hole and riser for the molten metal should be cut with a piece of brass tubing although any hollow tube having thin walls may be used (Fig. 199). The sprue hole cutter is pushed down through the sand at the place where the sprues are desired (see Fig. 215). Pack the sand carefully about the top of the sprue so that no loose particles will enter the mold. If the top of the hole is slightly enlarged at this time it will be easier to pour the molten metal.

The cope should now be lifted and set aside. This operation requires considerable care to make sure that it is lifted straight up in such a way that the sand will not be broken. Dampen the surface of the mold slightly around the patterns to strengthen the edges (Fig. 216), using a bulb sponge (Fig. 201). Drive a sharp pin into the pattern and rap lightly in all directions until the pattern is loose. Then lift the pattern out, being sure not to break the mold (Fig. 217). The gates leading from the sprues to the mold should be cut (Fig. 218) with a thin piece of sheet metal (Fig. 204) bent in the shape of a U. By cutting away from the mold and toward the sprue the danger of dropping sand where it will injure the appearance of the casting will be avoided. Pack the sand thoroughly in the bottom of the gates and sprues, and using a small hand bellows (Fig. 202), blow out any loose particles which may have accidently dropped into the mold. Replace the cope after carefully blowing out the sprue holes. A weight placed upon the top of the cope will eliminate any danger of metal running out between the two parts of the flask.

Enough metal should be melted to fill both molds and sprues. It is essential that sufficient metal be used, as a poor casting is the almost inevitable result of not filling the sprues completely. The pewter should be poured as soon as it will slightly char a pine stick (this temperature will show a pyrometer reading of from 450 to 500 degrees). As soon as the metal has reached the correct temperature skim the dross from the top and pour as rapidly as possible (Fig. 219). A sand mold cools very quickly and such small castings as the door knocker may be removed as soon as the metal is solid in the sprues.

Finishing. After the castings have been cleaned of sand by brushing or washing, the sprues and gates should be removed with a hack, coping, or jeweler's saw. If there is a thin fin of metal at the place where the two parts of the mold came together this may be removed with a knife or jeweler's saw, and any rough places smoothed with a file. It will probably be necessary to file all surfaces if a bright finish is desired. It is suggested that the clapper be finished all over, and that only the oval of the back plate be so treated. Filing should be followed first by fine (No. 00) emery cloth, and then by either tripoli or pumice if a buffing wheel is available. If it is necessary to finish by hand, a satin finish may be obtained by rubbing with pumice on a cloth or stiff brush. Number 00 steel wool will give a fairly satisfactory bright surface.

Fig. 220—Cored Statuette

Before the final polish is given, the pieces of brass on the front of the plate and the back of the clapper should be fitted. In the knocker shown in Fig. 192, the brass was cut from a $\frac{3}{16}$ in. $\times$ $\frac{1}{2}$ in. strip, but other available thicknesses might be used. Cut the brass to the correct shape and file the grooves in the knocker to fit. Then, using a pewter solder of low melting point and being careful to keep the point of the blow-pipe flame directed upon the brass, sweat the pieces into place. Also sweat flat-headed brass machine screws (or if these are not available, flat-headed stove bolts) on the back of the plate for attaching the knocker to the door. Give the work a final cleaning and polish with rouge or crocus.

How to Cast a Cored Figure in a Plaster Mold. A project of a type to offer a real challenge to the home craftsman or the industrial arts student is shown in Fig. 220. A model of an original small sculpture should be used if possible. If this is not available, most homes have numerous statuettes in porcelain, clay, plaster, wood, or metal that may be reproduced. Many of these figures have only a most ordinary appearance in their original form, but show a real richness when cast in pewter. Since most figures of this sort require too much metal if cast solid, a core is usually required.

A plaster cast for the outside of the figure is first constructed, using the technique described in the making of the candlestick (see Chapter 6). In some cases such molds may be made in only two pieces as shown in Fig. 221. Several pieces may be necessary for other patterns. Fig. 222 shows such a mold with the pieces disassembled. The following procedure is employed where the multiple mold is required: Examine the original carefully, marking lightly on the surface those sections which will "draw" without breaking the cast. Build a wall around one of these parts with thin strips of plasticene and fill with plaster to a depth of about an inch. Remove the wax and build a wall around an adjoining section, allowing the part already cast to act as one wall. Apply a soap sizing on all parts where the plaster comes together. Match pins should be inserted wherever they will not restrict the separation of the parts. Continue walling in and pouring one section after the other until the whole mold is completed. After the mold has had a chance to thoroughly dry, the pattern is removed and the inside lined to a depth of about $\frac{1}{8}$ to $\frac{3}{16}$ of an inch with plasticene or modeling wax. Any parts of the mold to cast solid should be filled completely (Fig. 223).

A frame of wire is constructed which will pass through the center of the hollow part of the mold and support any long, slender parts of the core which might otherwise be broken. The ends of this wire should pass through the wax and into the plaster at one or two points which will not show prominently on the surface of the casting (see Fig. 224). These ends support the armature (as the wire frame is called) laterally, while wires across the base of the mold suspend it until the mold is poured. It will be found worth while to spend considerable time in placing these supporting wires so that the core may be held rigidly in place. After the armature has been placed in position in one-half of the mold, the other half (or the base piece in the case of a multiple mold), is added to complete the mold. Mix enough plaster of Paris to fill the figure, and pour it inside of the wax around the armature. When the mixture has had time to set, open the mold, remove the wax, and the core which now covers the wire armature is ready for drying. Too much stress cannot be laid upon the need for *thorough* drying of both mold and core. The slightest amount of moisture in either is likely to result in steam pockets which will prevent the mold from filling, causing holes to form in the casting.

When it is certain that both molds and core are thoroughly dry, cut the gates for pouring, and also cut vents to parts where air may be trapped. The entire mold should then be given a coat of smoke or black lead to aid in removing the casting. All parts of the mold and core are next assembled and firmly tied together. Heat sufficient metal to fill the mold and pour quickly. Keep the pouring gate filled with molten metal as long as it continues to shrink.

Give the metal sufficient time to cool and remove the outer mold. The core may be removed with a scratch awl or similar sharp instrument, as shown

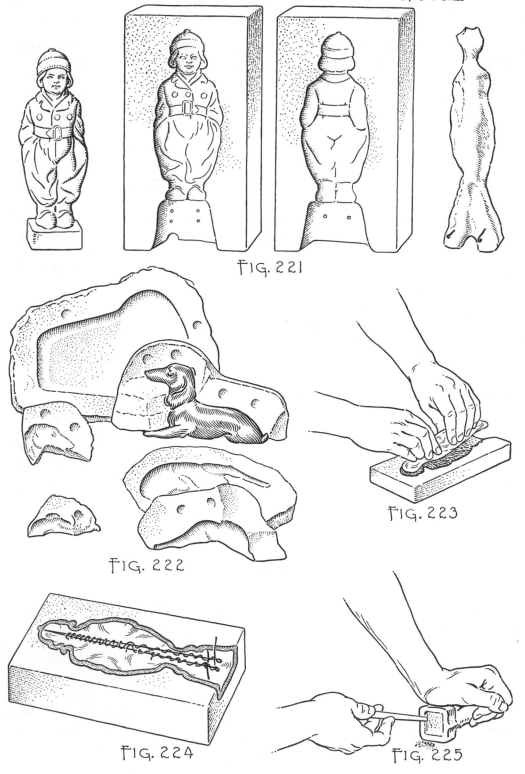

FIG. 221

FIG. 222

FIG. 223

FIG. 224

FIG. 225

in Fig. 225. Cleaning up and finishing the figure are now accomplished in the usual manner. (See p. 94).

Cuttle-Bone Casting. Jewelers and workers in gold and other precious metals have used cuttle-fish bone for making molds since very early times. Small and intricate parts and pieces were commonly made by this method. The possibilities of using this medium as a mold for pewter casting seem, however, to have been consistently overlooked. Figs. 226 and 227 show a few of the numerous possible applications of cuttle bones. Watch-fobs, badges, and various types of insignia lend themselves to this means of reproduction.

Cuttle-fish bones of a grade suitable for making castings may be purchased from almost any firm specializing in metal-craft or jewelry supplies. The same material is used as a food for birds, and suitable pieces may sometimes be found at pet shops. The bones come in a variety of sizes listed as "small," "medium" and "large." For ordinary work the medium size is most desirable.

It will be noted that the molds made from this material may be of two or more pieces. A small watch fob (Fig. 227) illustrates the making of a two-piece mold.

Making the Mold. Select a sound bone of appropriate size, and with a jeweler's saw or hack-saw, cut the bone into two parts which should be approximately equal in size, as illustrated by Fig. 228. Note that one side of each piece is soft and spongy, while the other is covered with a hard, bony structure. Place the soft side of each piece on a flat piece of very fine sand paper (preferably 6/0) and sand down with a circular motion until a perfectly flat and true surface has been obtained (see Fig. 229). Jewelers and goldsmiths use a special stone for this purpose. Try the two pieces together to make sure that they will match when the mold is completed.

Lay the pattern which has been selected on one piece to make sure where the limits of the mold will come. After preparing three short pointed pegs (about $\frac{3}{16}$ of an inch in length), insert the end which is not sharpened into one piece of the bone in some part that will not interfere with the pattern. To make sure that these pieces will remain in place it is well to place a drop of silicate of soda around each one and allow it to dry. Next place the two parts of the bone with the sawed edges even, and press until the flat surfaces come together. The holes made by these pegs now provide a means whereby the two pieces may be taken apart and replaced as often as desired.

The pattern is placed in position upon one of the pieces and pressed firmly into the bone until about half the thickness of the fob is below the surface (Fig. 230). Next place the other half of the bone in position, lining it

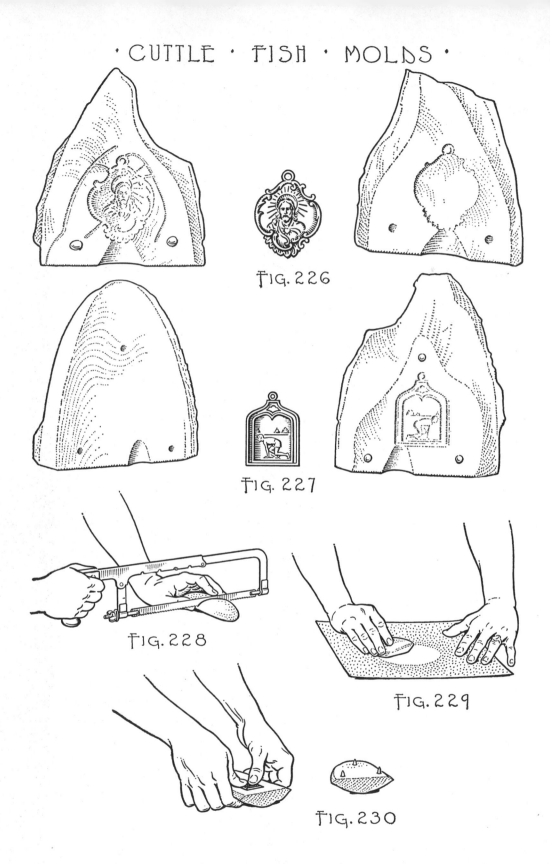

FIG. 226

FIG. 227

FIG. 228

FIG. 229

FIG. 230

up carefully by means of the matching pegs. Hold the mold firmly between the palms of the hands, place the hands between the knees, and exert a steady even pressure on the two pieces until the flat surfaces come together as depicted in Fig. 231. It is very important that the pressure be applied evenly over the surface of the mold, otherwise the bone will be cracked. If it should be cracked in spite of all reasonable care, the half of the mold which is not broken may be saved by matching it with another piece of similar size. Separate the mold and remove the pattern. It will usually fall out if the mold is inverted. If it does not, a knife point or other sharp instrument may be used to loosen it.

The pouring gate is easily cut into the mold with a sharp knife (Fig. 232). Make the gate as large as is possible without defacing the appearance of the casting. All parts of the mold which are likely to trap air should be vented by scratching fine lines (about the size of an ordinary needle) across the face of the bone radiating from the mold.

The surface of the mold must now be treated to withstand the heat of the molten metal. First mix a strong solution of borax ("Twenty Mule Team" will do). This solution should be painted over the face of the mold with a very fine camel-hair brush, being sure not to disturb any fine detail (Fig. 233). The borax is followed while still wet with a coating of a fifty-fifty solution of silicate of soda and water. Just before this mixture becomes entirely dry the pattern should be returned to the mold and the two parts pressed firmly together. If the procedure has been carried out correctly up to this point the mold will present a very sharp and smoothly polished appearance when the pattern is removed. All moisture should evaporate by allowing the parts to stand open for several days. A slow heat may, however, be used to hasten the process.

The pouring of the mold presents some problems not met in ordinary pewter casting. The fact that most articles which lend themselves to this type of casting are rather small and are likely to have thin places in them, makes it necessary to heat the metal to a considerably higher temperature than for larger and thicker castings. The metal should be heated until a piece of dry paper pushed into it will burst into flame. The two parts of the mold may be held together with fine wire while the metal is being poured, but some method should be provided for rocking the mold slightly as the metal enters. Some craftsmen prefer to hold the mold in the hand, as in Fig. 234, carefully keeping it tipped to prevent the hot metal from being spilled on the fingers. If the mold is well prepared and handled gently it is possible to make several castings from one mold.

The making of a three-piece mold for the ring shown in Fig. 235, requires a slightly different technique. Two pieces of bone should be smoothed off on

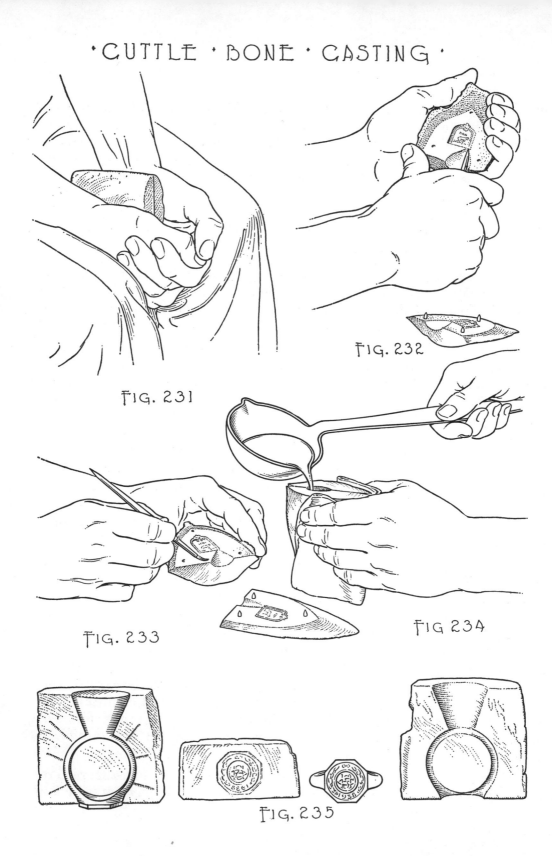

FIG. 231

FIG. 232

FIG. 233

FIG 234

FIG. 235

the stone or sandpaper as just described. Press the ring into one piece with the setting or seal near the top surface. Press the other part of the bone in place, entirely enclosing the ring. Then, holding the pieces carefully together, even off the top edges where the bone was sawed apart, and also the two sides. Now if guide marks are placed on the sides, it will be possible to take the pieces apart and replace them in the same position. When the mold is taken apart it will be found that there is a complete impression of the ring, but the seal or inscription on the top has, of course, been scraped out. The top of the mold should be carefully sanded down until the opening where the inscription or seal should come appears as an open space in the bone. The ring is then replaced in the mold and another piece of bone which has been previously prepared to fit the top of the other two pieces, is pressed down upon the mold until a close joint is formed. Witness marks should be placed on the sides of all three pieces in order that the third piece may be replaced in exact position.

The pouring gate for a mold of this kind is usually made at the bottom of the ring as shown in Fig. 235. Small radiating vents should be made in the face of the bone, and the surface then treated as described in the case of the two-piece mold. When completely dry the pieces should be carefully wired together for pouring.

Rings and pieces of jewelry of this type, while not particularly durable, are cheap; and it has been found that they are greatly appreciated by younger children. They have the advantage of not tarnishing easily.

Pewter Spoons from Metal Molds. Pewter spoons were once made in great numbers. Due to wear they were frequently recast, and for this reason, while pewter spoons are not uncommon, marked examples by known makers are difficult to find. The spoon-mold was a common household utensil during Colonial days, and many early families recast their own spoons. For the craftsman who wishes to revive the art of spoon molding, the fabrication of a mold from aluminum or bronze is an intriguing possibility.

Care should be exercised in selecting the spoon from which the mold is to be made to see if it will lend itself to casting in pewter. The lines should be relatively simple and plain, and the spoon should be thick enough to provide a mold that will fill. The ordinary stamped spoons are rarely heavy enough to serve well as a model. If a real pewter spoon can be obtained it makes an ideal pattern. Even if parts are somewhat worn, the form may be restored by carefully cutting away portions of the plaster mold to renew the original shape. If an original pewter model is not available, a suitable substitute may be found in composition spoons, or a pattern may be carved or modeled.

A layer of plasticene somewhat larger than the size of the spoon should be rolled out to a thickness at about half an inch and placed upon a piece of

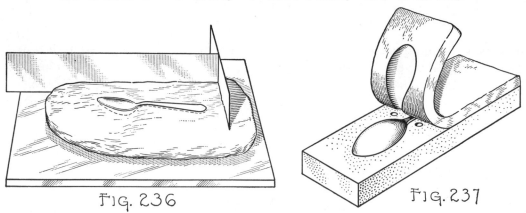

Fig. 236

Fig. 237

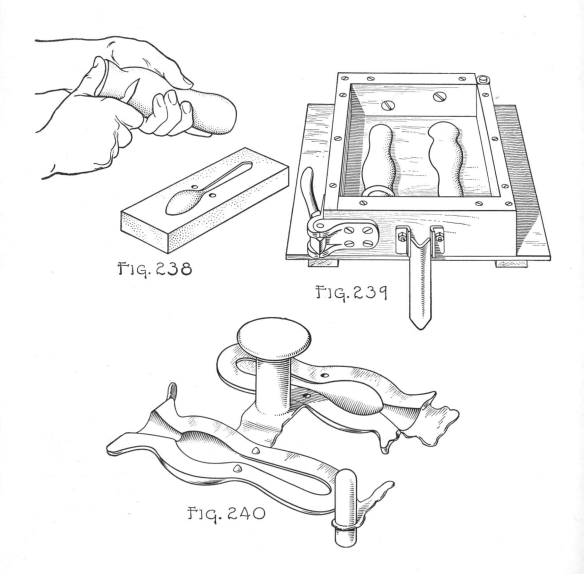

Fig. 238

Fig. 239

Fig. 240

glass. The spoon is used as a pattern, and is pressed into the plasticene up to the parting line. The top surface of the wax is cut away to conform roughly with the contour of the spoon (see Fig. 236). A better appearing mold will result if the surface is shaped with a sharp knife and smoothed with the fingers moistened with glycerine. Strips of sheet metal should be placed around the spoon, and pushed down through the plasticene to the glass. At least half an inch of space should be left between the spoon and the side of the mold at all points, and *at least an inch at the tip of the spoon where the metal is to be poured.*

Mix the plaster according to the directions given for the Ship's Candlestick in Chapter 6, and pour so that all parts of the spoon are covered to a depth of at least half an inch. Allow the mold to set for at least two or three hours before removing the form. It may be necessary to cut the plasticene loose from the glass by the use of a fine wire or a thin piece of sheet metal, after which the wax may be peeled away from the plaster as shown in Fig. 237. The spoon should now be removed from the mold, and the surface carefully examined for holes caused by air bubbles. If any air holes are found they may be filled with soft plaster, and the surface smoothed before the spoon is replaced in the mold.

The top surface of the mold should be covered with soap sizing or with a special parting solution, and after three or four holes for matching are made in the surface close to the edge of the pattern, the sheet metal strips are replaced and secured in place with plasticene. Replace the spoon in the mold, mix a new supply of plaster as before, and pour it over the mold. Be sure to jar the glass repeatedly to remove all air bubbles from the solution.

When the second part of the mold has had an opportunity to set, the strips of sheet metal may be removed, the wax gathered up, and the mold separated. The process up to this point has been that of making an ordinary plaster mold. However, a new technique is now introduced. Before the plaster has had a chance to dry thoroughly, the excess plaster should be carved away with a sharp knife until about one-half an inch remains around all parts of the spoon (Fig. 238). Care should be taken that the carving provides sufficient draft for the plaster mold to be used as a pattern and drawn out of the sand when it is molded. It should be noted that a large section is left for a pouring gate near the tip of the spoon.

Sand molds are now made, using each piece of the plaster casts just described as a separate pattern as in Fig. 239. The greatest care should be taken not to ram the mold too hard as much force is sure to break the plaster. It is also well to make certain that there are no hollow places under the casts as they lay on the mold board. If any hollows are discovered they should be built up with sand before the molding is begun. When the molds are complete and ready to pour, a supply of scrap aluminum should be melted in a crucible or an iron ladle. Old automobile pistons or cylinder heads make an excellent alloy for this purpose, and may be secured at most junk dealers. The aluminum may be melted in a regular melting or heat-treating furnace, in an ordinary coal forge, or in the home furnace. As aluminum is spoiled for casting purposes by over-heating, it should be poured as soon as it reaches a completely liquid state. Further heating only tends to imperfect casting. When the castings have had time enough to solidify (about four to eight minutes, according to size), they may be removed from the sand, the gates and risers removed, and the cleaning up process started, their appearance at this stage being shown in Fig. 240. The only part of the mold which must be smooth is that which comes in contact with the pewter as the spoon is cast. All rough places should be carefully removed with riffle files or with small chisels and scrapers made to fit into special places. Emery and crocus cloth may be used for the final cleaning, or the mold may be buffed with rouge to give a polished finish.

If the faces of the mold do not fit tightly they should be worked down until no metal can possibly leak out. This operation is best performed by covering the surface of one part with bearing blue, then fitting the parts together and pressing them tightly into place. The parts which should be worked down by filing or scraping will then appear blue on the uncoated face, This process of marking and fitting must be repeated alternately until the mold is tight at all points.

When completely fitted and ready for pouring, the inside should be thoroughly coated with carbon from a flame and heated to a temperature which is only slightly below that of the pewter to be poured. Clamp the parts tightly with C-clamps or hold with tongs and pour the metal rapidly. Be sure that the pouring gate is filled completely. The mold should be rocked slightly if possible as the metal is poured. This motion helps to insure a full mold. If the metal does not fill the mold smoothly it is sometimes helpful to coat the inside surfaces with a traditional mixture of egg white and yellow ochre, or with black lead or graphite. Each of these treatments has been found helpful under various conditions.

The method described in making this spoon mold may also be used in making metal molds for other purposes. For example, one frequently sees a small tray, a plate, or other utensil which could be cast if a mold were available. By covering the outside surface with plaster, and making an aluminum casting in sand from the resulting plaster pattern, a mold suitable for the purpose will result.

Slush Casting. A method of making hollow castings from pewter, lead, and other soft alloys, but one which seems to have escaped notice, is known as "slush" casting. Commercially, the process consists of pouring the molten metal into prepared molds made from "gun metal," and pouring out the center before it has had time to solidify, much like slip casting in pottery. This method produces a casting which conforms exactly to the mold on the outside, but which, except for a thin wall of metal, is entirely hollow. The application of this process to the making of spouts, handles, knobs, salt shakers, and similar articles will be at once apparent.

While bronze is undoubtedly the best metal for these molds, most school and home workshops are not equipped to melt it. Aluminum works almost as well, and its melting point is much lower. It conducts the heat away from the metal somewhat more rapidly than bronze, hence the casting must be done faster.

Fig. 241—Patterns and Plaster Casts for Salt Shakers

Making the Pattern. Any pattern suitable for plaster casting may be used to make a mold for slush casting. It may be chosen from porcelain or wood examples, as illustrated by the salt shakers shown in Fig. 241. It might be made from a metal casting or from a clay, soap, or wax model as in Fig. 249. An example of how the spout for a teapot might be modeled is indicated in Fig. 242. A full-size drawing of the desired part should be laid out on tracing paper, a piece of modeling wax or plasticene of approximately the correct width, thickness, and length secured, and the shape of the spout marked upon the surface of the modeling material by laying the tracing paper upon it and pricking holes around the outline with a needle. The outline should be cut with a sharp knife, and trimmed roughly to the correct shape. This blank

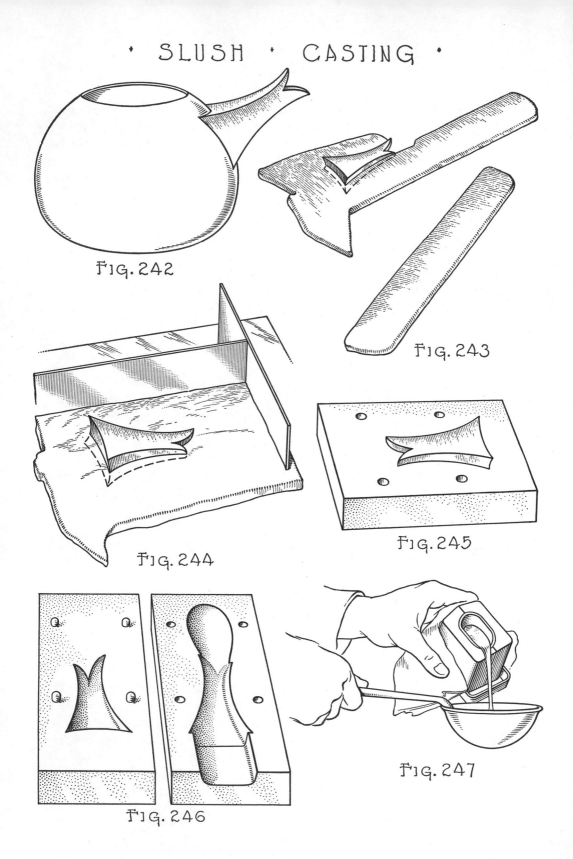

· SLUSH · CASTING ·

FIG. 242

FIG. 243

FIG. 244

FIG. 245

FIG. 246

FIG. 247

should then be placed upon the body of the teapot in the position where the spout will be fastened. It should be modeled to exact size and shape, using the fingers and a knife or modeling tools. The final form should be smoothed by rubbing with the fingers moistened slightly with glycerine.

Making the Plaster Mold. If the pattern has been modeled as described above it may now be cut loose from the side of the teapot by drawing a fine wire between them. Mark the center line of the spout to indicate the parting line. Prepare strips of plasticene approximately an inch wide and a quarter of an inch thick, and press the edge of these pieces against the pattern so that their upper surfaces are even with the parting line. Half of the pattern now projects above the plasticene as shown in Fig. 243. Next lay the pattern down upon a piece of glass and pack pieces of plasticene under it until the parting line on the pattern is in a horizontal position. Also, level up the strips of plasticene by placing other pieces beneath them. The sides of the mold should next be formed by placing pieces of sheet metal around the pattern as in Fig. 244, or if the mold is too irregular to lend itself to the regular mold the sides may be formed of additional strips of plasticene. The plaster is poured in the usual manner, being sure to fill the mold to at least ⅜ of an inch over the top of the highest part of the pattern.

Fig. 248—Examples of Slush Casting

When the plaster has had an opportunity to set, turn the mold over and remove the plasticene which surrounds the pattern (Fig. 245). Level any irregular places on the top surface of the plaster, make the necessary holes for match marks, size the surface of the mold, replace the strips of sheet metal or plasticene, and pour the second half of the mold. After allowing sufficient time for this part to set, the two halves may be separated and the pattern removed.

The pouring gate should next be cut at the large end of the spout (Fig. 246). This gate should be almost as large as the end of the spout itself, leaving only a small ridge to show where the excess metal is to be removed. A reservoir should be carved in the plaster at the small end of the mold so that the spout can be cast hollow its entire length. Fig. 246 shows suitable shapes for these openings, which may be made with a woodworker's gouge. After one side has been carved, a small amount of cup grease should be spread upon its top surface, and the two halves pressed together. The grease will show on the

· ADDITIONAL · CAST · PROJECTS ·

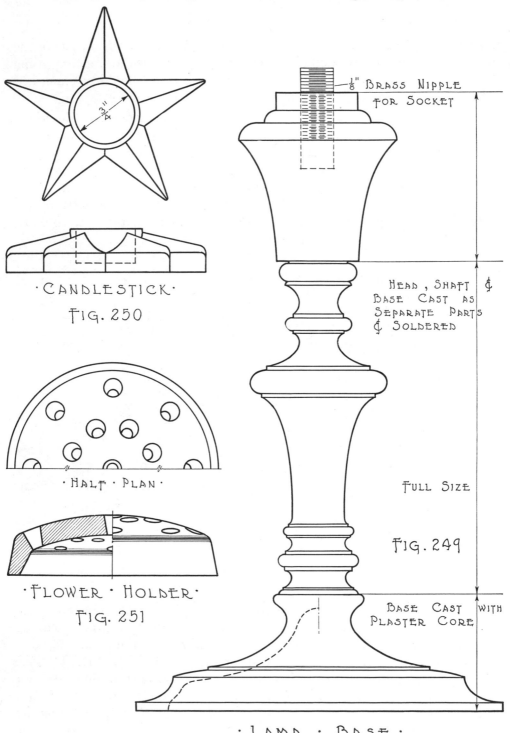

· CANDLESTICK ·

FIG. 250

· HALF · PLAN ·

· FLOWER · HOLDER ·

FIG. 251

$\frac{1}{8}$" BRASS NIPPLE
FOR SOCKET

HEAD, SHAFT &
BASE CAST AS
SEPARATE PARTS
& SOLDERED

FULL SIZE

FIG. 249

BASE CAST WITH
PLASTER CORE

· LAMP · BASE ·
(AFTER EARLY OIL LAMP)

uncarved surface, making it possible to cut both to the same contour. Carve a slight draft on the sides of the mold to enable them to draw away from the sand mold.

The plaster casts should be molded in sand as described in the case of the door knocker. Care should be taken to make the gates and sprues extra large to compensate for the excessive shrinkage of aluminum. Avoid overheating the aluminum if a sharp, solid casting is desired. When a suitable casting of each half has been secured, remove the sprues and smooth the inside of the mold with files and emery cloth. The joint where the two parts of the mold come together should be examined, and if any considerable opening is found, the parts should be fitted with file and scraper, using bearing blue or similar material to reveal the high spots.

Fig. 252—Soap Carving for Pattern

It requires only a minimum of practice before a mold of this type may be used to produce excellent results. To warm the mold, heat the casting pewter until it is thoroughly liquid, pour one casting into the mold and let it become solid. Remove this from the mold and quickly pour another, but this time as soon as the metal starts to solidify around the edges, pour the metal which is still molten at the center back into the ladle, as illustrated in Fig. 247. A few attempts will show the amount of time required to allow the metal to stand in the mold before the slush is poured out. Fig. 248 shows some of the possibilities in slush casting. Once the mold is made, piece after piece can be turned out in rapid succession. The making of Christmas presents or school or personal souvenirs by this method presents many interesting possibilities.

Further suggestions for pewter casting are indicated by the lamp base Fig. 249, the candlestick Fig. 250, and the flower holder Fig. 251. Incidentally, soap carvings offer a latitude of opportunity in the fabrication of unique patterns for pewter novelties, as may be gathered from Fig. 252.

Chapter Eleven

Spinning Low Forms

*M*ANY INTERESTING and valuable articles of general cylindrical form may be made by the process of spinning. Briefly, spinning consists of forcing a circular disc of metal to fit around a form or chuck which is revolving on a lathe.

The Lathe. A lathe is the first requirement. It must be provided with bearings of sufficient strength to stand up under the fairly heavy thrusting force exerted on them by the spinning operation. One should inquire of the lathe manufacturer as to its adaptability for this purpose before starting to work, although most manufacturers of lathes are now equipping their product with suitable bearings. The lathe should have variable speeds.

Special Equipment for the Lathe. Among accessories of the lathe a special tool rest is desirable. Fig. 253 shows several types that are suitable. One of the most important accessories is the special revolving dead center. While a simple block of wood lubricated with soap or grease will serve the purpose, work may be done with more facility if a revolving center is fitted to the lathe. Several types are shown in Figs. 254, 255, 256, and 257. Some lathes are now provided with these centers by the manufacturer.

Tools. The professional spinner is equipped with tools of steel made in many shapes for various processes. Examination of a trade catalog will show these tools, and they may be used if desired (Fig. 259). Fortunately for the pewter craftsman, entirely effective tools may be made of wood with little or no cost. A common broomstick, or better, an ash or hickory hammer or sledge handle of 18- or 24-inch length will serve the purpose with complete satisfaction. Fig. 258 suggests a few shapes for common use. Others will be found desirable as the worker engages in making more complex articles.

Chucks. Most chucks for ordinary work are made of maple, birch, or beech. Dogwood is excellent for articles up to six or eight inches in diameter. Porous woods, or those with considerable difference in the hardness of spring and summer rings, should be avoided, as they will leave marks of the grain on the soft metal. Chucks may be made of aluminum, cast iron, or other metals if great accuracy is desired, or if quantity production is to be carried on.

The chuck may be mounted on the lathe in one of several ways. If enough face plates are available that the chuck will not need to be removed before it has served its purpose, it may be fastened to one of the face plates, using as many and as heavy screws as the holes in the plate will permit.

· LATHE · EQUIPMENT · FOR · SPINNING ·

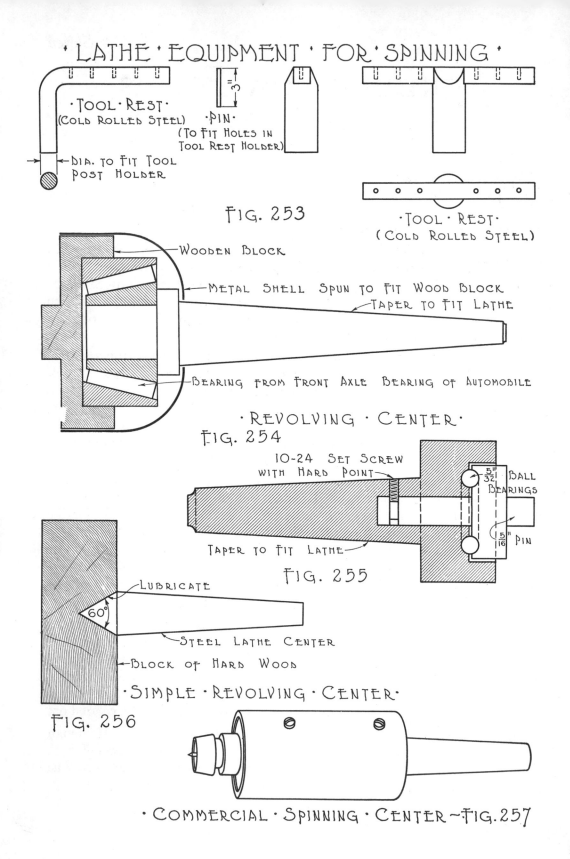

·TOOL·REST·
(COLD ROLLED STEEL)

·PIN·
(TO FIT HOLES IN
TOOL REST HOLDER)

DIA. TO FIT TOOL
POST HOLDER

FIG. 253

·TOOL·REST·
(COLD ROLLED STEEL)

WOODEN BLOCK

METAL SHELL SPUN TO FIT WOOD BLOCK
TAPER TO FIT LATHE

BEARING FROM FRONT AXLE BEARING OF AUTOMOBILE

· REVOLVING · CENTER ·
FIG. 254

10-24 SET SCREW
WITH HARD POINT

$\frac{5}{32}$" BALL BEARINGS

$\frac{5}{16}$" PIN

TAPER TO FIT LATHE

FIG. 255

LUBRICATE

60°

STEEL LATHE CENTER

BLOCK OF HARD WOOD

·SIMPLE·REVOLVING·CENTER·

FIG. 256

· COMMERCIAL · SPINNING · CENTER ~ FIG. 257

SPINNING · TOOLS ·

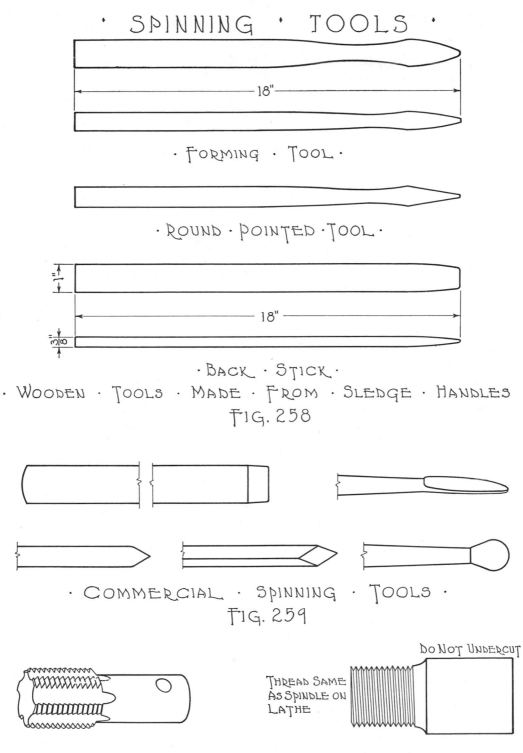

· FORMING · TOOL ·

· ROUND · POINTED · TOOL ·

· BACK · STICK ·

· WOODEN · TOOLS · MADE · FROM · SLEDGE · HANDLES ·

FIG. 258

· COMMERCIAL · SPINNING · TOOLS ·

FIG. 259

· CHUCK · TAP ·

FIG. 260

THREAD SAME AS SPINDLE ON LATHE

DO NOT UNDERCUT

· THREADED · PLUG ·

FIG. 261

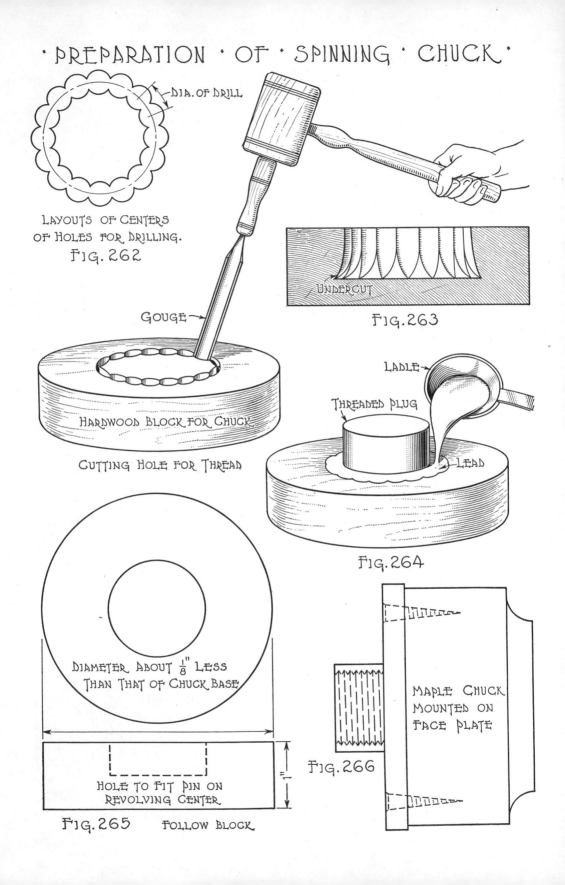

· PREPARATION · OF · SPINNING · CHUCK ·

DIA. OF DRILL

LAYOUTS OF CENTERS
OF HOLES FOR DRILLING.
FIG. 262

UNDERCUT

FIG. 263

GOUGE

HARDWOOD BLOCK FOR CHUCK

CUTTING HOLE FOR THREAD

LADLE

THREADED PLUG

LEAD

FIG. 264

DIAMETER ABOUT $\frac{1}{8}$" LESS
THAN THAT OF CHUCK BASE

HOLE TO FIT PIN ON
REVOLVING CENTER

FIG. 265   FOLLOW BLOCK

MAPLE CHUCK
MOUNTED ON
FACE PLATE

FIG. 266

Another method is to cut threads directly in the chuck to fit it to the spindle. Bore a hole to the root diameter of the spindle, fill with machine oil, and allow it to stand overnight. If a metal working lathe is used, the chuck may be centered in a lathe chuck and threads cut as they would be in metal. Taps may be purchased by which these threads may be cut by hand (Fig. 260).

A very effective method is that of casting the threads in lead in the chuck. For this purpose a threaded plug must be made or purchased, with threads identical with those of the lathe spindle, as pictured in Fig. 261.

Scribe a circle around the center of the chuck, about one-half an inch larger in diameter than the threading plug. Lay off centers for holes (Fig. 262) and drill to a depth slightly greater than the length of the threaded part of the plug. If this operation is carefully performed the center can easily be removed.

Gouge out the thin wood, retaining the thicker projecting parts, then undercut by completely removing sections of some of these below the surface of the block as illustrated in Fig. 263. This treatment is designed to form a hollow to hold the lead firmly in the chuck.

Warm the threading plug and give it a coat of carbon by holding in the sooty flame of a torch or candle. Center the plug in the hole of the chuck and pour lead around it (Fig. 264). When this lead cools, back the plug out and mount the chuck on the lathe.

Follow-Blocks. Each spinning job should have a follow-block turned from soft wood. The follow-block may be bored or turned to fit the projecting pin on the revolving center as in Fig. 265, or if there is no pin, a brad may be driven in and clipped off with about one-fourth of an inch projecting. The diameter is usually just enough smaller than the base of the chuck to permit the forming tool to reach to the base. If much smaller than the chuck, a ridge will form on the metal around the follow-block. The final shaping may be done by putting the block on the revolving center and bringing it in firm contact with the chuck, thereby enabling turning tools to be used on it.

Coaster. The chuck for the coaster (Fig. 266) should be turned to the shape shown by the drawing, and of a size suitable for a set of glasses. Rough out the chuck with a turner's gouge, then turn to shape with skew and round-nose tools. The chuck should taper very slightly down to the edge of the curved section. Sand very smoothly.

Determination of the right size to cut the discs of pewter is partly a matter of experience and practice. In theory the metal should be cut to a size that will provide the same number of square inches in the disc as there will be in the finished product. In practice, this size is almost impossible to

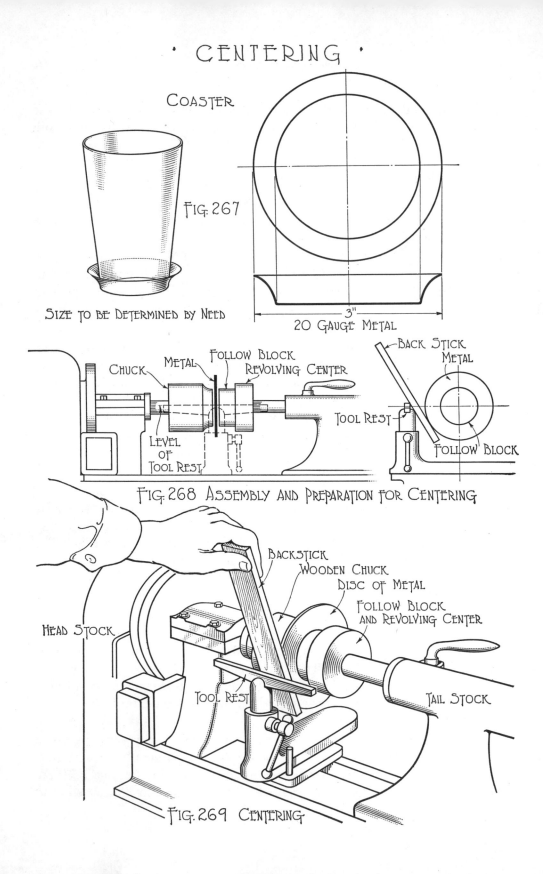

· CENTERING ·

COASTER

FIG. 267

SIZE TO BE DETERMINED BY NEED

3"
20 GAUGE METAL

CHUCK   METAL   FOLLOW BLOCK
REVOLVING CENTER

BACK STICK
METAL

TOOL REST

LEVEL
OF
TOOL REST

FOLLOW BLOCK

FIG. 268 ASSEMBLY AND PREPARATION FOR CENTERING

BACKSTICK
WOODEN CHUCK
DISC OF METAL
FOLLOW BLOCK
AND REVOLVING CENTER

HEAD STOCK

TOOL REST

TAIL STOCK

FIG. 269 CENTERING

compute on some articles, so a rule of thumb method is employed. To determine the radius of the disc to be cut, draw a straight line, or chord, from the edge of the base to the edge of the rim on the drawing of the article. Now add this length to the radius of the base for the result. It will usually be found that this length is greater than necessary, except for objects with a very small raised edge. Experience will show just about how much to reduce this figure to avoid using too large a piece. It is undesirable to have the diameter any greater than necessary, since the difficulty of spinning increases somewhat in geometric ratio to the height of the article and the diameter of the disc. Fig. 267 will illustrate the method of determining the size as just described. Another method is to add the largest diameter to the height. The sum is the diameter of the disc.

Centering. Place one of the discs of pewter against the form and set the follow-block against it just tightly enough to hold the metal in place. Shift the disc until it seems to be centered as nearly as the eye can judge (Fig. 268). This will suffice for getting started, but the metal must run perfectly true before actual spinning is begun. Set the tool rest parallel to the lathe bed, and back from the disc a distance of two or three inches. Set a strong flat piece of hard wood over the tool rest and under the disc and hold it firmly against the rim of the metal as shown in Fig. 269. Stand to one side of the plane of the disc, and start the lathe at a speed of about 400 r.p.m. (Do not permit observers to stand in line with the disc.) Loosen the tail stock slightly so that the metal will respond to the touch of the stick. If the tool is held with a firm steady grip, the metal will quickly center itself. Now tighten the tail stock quickly so that the metal will be held firmly. If the disc gets far out of center, do not continue, but stop the lathe and center it again as at first. If difficulty is encountered in keeping the metal running true, put a little rosin on the end of the chuck.

Catching the Foot. The forming tool should be picked up at once and pressure applied at the base of the chuck to cause the metal to catch just over the foot of the chuck far enough to hold. Fig. 270 will show the position of the tool and the direction of pressure. In performing this operation, put the tool over the rest, which has been turned at an angle to the lathe bed, and at the left of the pin. Apply the point of the tool to the metal at a point just at the base of the form, and somewhat below the center of revolution. Pull the handle of the tool to the right and downward. This action will force the metal to yield enough to assume a shape about as shown in Fig. 271.

Trimming. By this time the metal may not be running entirely true, and it should be trimmed before any further spinning is done. Hold the form-

· TRIMMING · & · DRAWING-IN ·

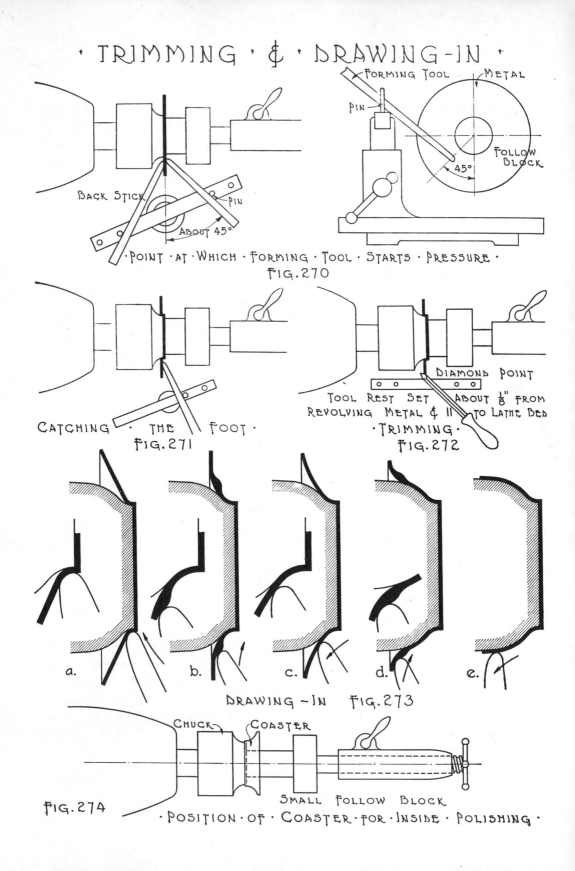

FORMING TOOL · · METAL

PIN

FOLLOW BLOCK

45°

BACK STICK · PIN

ABOUT 45°

· POINT · AT · WHICH · FORMING · TOOL · STARTS · PRESSURE ·
FIG. 270

CATCHING · THE · FOOT ·
FIG. 271

DIAMOND POINT

TOOL REST SET ABOUT ⅛" FROM
REVOLVING METAL & ‖ TO LATHE BED
· TRIMMING ·
FIG. 272

a.   b.   c.   d.   e.

DRAWING ~IN   FIG. 273

CHUCK   COASTER

SMALL FOLLOW BLOCK

FIG. 274
· POSITION · OF · COASTER · FOR · INSIDE · POLISHING ·

ing tool on the right side of the metal, and the back stick opposite it on the left side. Apply pressure with both, moving them out to the rim, thus forcing the metal to run between them in a flat plane. Move the tool rest around in front of the disc, and within one-eighth of an inch of the edge. Cautiously apply the trimming tool to the edge, holding it firmly on the tool rest. Trim just enough metal to reach the point where a thin slice is being taken all the way around (Fig. 272). It will be well to wear goggles during this operation, or hold a flat stick above the trimming tool.

Using the Forming Tool. The disc is now ready for the final shaping. Move the tool rest back far enough to permit the forming tool to have room to move freely, and set it on an angle which will give support to the tool as it is forced against the metal. Be sure the rest is securely clamped. Run the lathe at a speed of 800 to 1200 r.p.m., the higher speeds being used on smaller discs of metal.

Place the forming tool over the rest, as before, and place the point about a quarter of an inch outside the base just formed (Fig. 270). Apply pressure, in the direction of the form and toward the base, forcing the metal to flow in front of the tool and toward the form. Move the tool out another short distance and repeat. If the metal shows any signs of buckling along the edge, place the back stick against the left side of the disc and force the metal to run between the stick and the forming tool. The back stick thus acts as a kind of flexible chuck which yields to the pressure of the forming tool, but which, by forcing the metal to pass between the two tools, keeps it straightened out. Force the metal tightly to the chuck and move the tool back and forth across the surface to even up the distribution of metal.

Finishing. Set the tool rest for trimming (Fig. 272) and trim the edge down to the chuck. Remove the tool rest and hold a small wad of fine steel wool against the revolving metal. The steel wool should be kept in motion with a light pressure. Follow the steel wool with tripoli or pumice and oil on a cloth. Do not apply much pressure, and be careful that no loose ends of cloth are free to catch. When tripoli or pumice are used the clothing should be protected against flying oil. The inside of the coaster can be polished in the same way by reversing it in the lathe (Fig. 274).

Ash Tray. The ash tray (Fig. 275) is representative of a great number of articles with rims larger in diameter than the bases, varying from about an inch up to several inches in height, and having tapering sides. Fig. 276 offers a diagrammatic method of determining the diameter of a metal disc required to spin such a form.

· FINDING · DIAMETER · OF · DISC ·

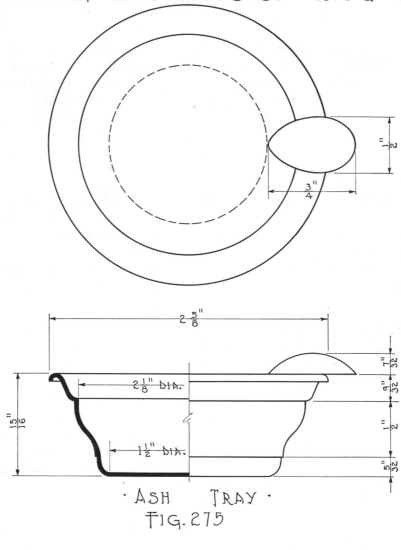

$2\frac{5}{8}''$

$2\frac{1}{8}''$ DIA.

$1\frac{1}{2}''$ DIA.

$\frac{15}{16}''$

$\frac{7}{32}''$

$\frac{9}{32}''$

$\frac{1}{2}''$

$\frac{5}{32}''$

$\frac{1}{2}''$

$\frac{3}{4}''$

· ASH   TRAY ·
FIG. 275

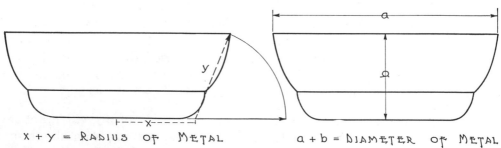

$x + y$ = RADIUS OF METAL $a + b$ = DIAMETER OF METAL

DIAGRAMMATIC · METHODS · OF · FINDING · DIAMETER
OF · METAL · DISC · REQUIRED · TO · SPIN · AN · OBJECT
FIG. 276

Turn a chuck for the bowl of the ash tray and reduce the diameter all over just enough to allow for 18- gauge metal to bring the over-all dimensions to those indicated on the drawing. Take care that the curves are smooth and regular, with no noticeable sharp projections, or flat parts. Prepare a follow-block slightly smaller than the base of the chuck and fit it to the revolving center. Proceed as before to center the metal, force it over the foot of the chuck, trim and straighten. Lubricate the surface of the metal by holding tallow or cup grease against it.

Fig. 277—Ash Tray

Forming. More difficulty will be encountered from this point on than was experienced in making the low-rimmed coaster. One might think that spinning such an article would be the very simple operation of starting the tool at the base, and pushing the metal to the chuck following its curve up to the rim. To thus push the metal would result in tearing it apart at a point about half an inch above the base. It should be understood that pushing the metal to the chuck by moving from base to rim does not affect the metal at the rim at first, so the metal must increase its length, from base to rim, while a consequent thinning is taking place. If the piece is an inch and a half or more in height the metal usually tears apart. To avoid this failure follow the diagram of Fig. 273. To understand this diagram, it must be remembered that the molecules of pewter flow in front of the tool like soft wax would do, and the metal can be moved from one part to another. Thus it may be seen that the tool brings metal from a point about half an inch from the base to a position nearer the base (Fig. 273 *b*). Then the disc is straightened out and the thickened portion is forced down to the chuck by the motion of the tool to the left (Fig. 273 *c*), which thins out the metal to the normal thickness. This process is repeated little by little until the entire form has been covered (Figs. 273 *a, b, d, e*). It will be noticed that the operation of forming causes the disc to curve toward the right. Before anything else is done place the back stick and forming tool about half an inch from the point where the metal

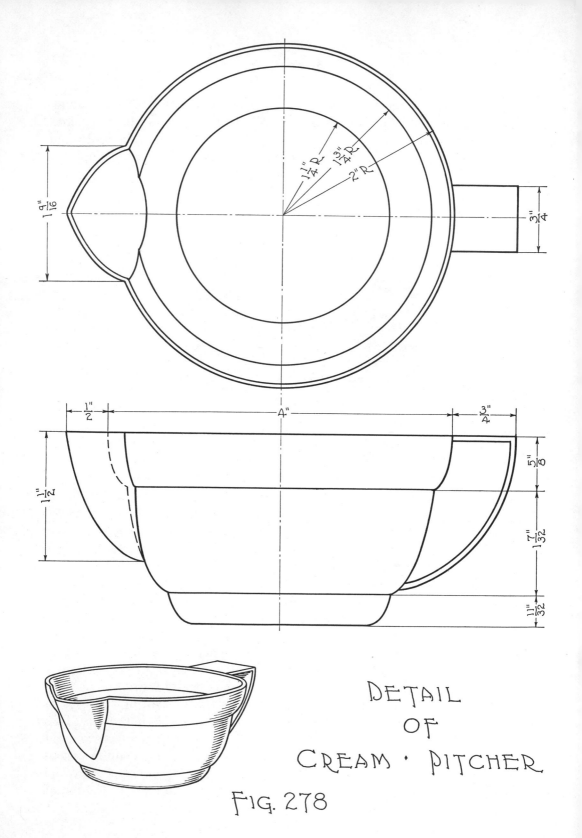

$1\frac{1}{4}$"R $1\frac{3}{4}$"R 2"R

$1\frac{9}{16}$"

$\frac{3}{4}$"

$\frac{1}{2}$" A" $\frac{3}{4}$"

$1\frac{1}{2}$" $\frac{5}{8}$"

$1\frac{7}{32}$"

$\frac{11}{32}$"

DETAIL
OF
CREAM · PITCHER

FIG. 278

touches the chuck and shape the metal back to the left, working out toward the rim, and causing it to gradually curve toward the chuck. This action will need to be repeated frequently.

Care must be observed to equalize pressure to avoid forming ridges and hollows, which may be detected by running the tips of the fingers over the surface, or by drawing the metal off the form and testing the thickness between thumb and finger. Trimming completes the shaping, after which the piece may be polished while on the lathe. Cut out the rests for the tray, bend them to shape, and solder in place.

Other articles similar to the ash tray (Fig. 277) include cream pitcher, shown in detail in Fig. 278, porringer (Fig. 157), bon-bon dish with cover, and card salver with cast feet.

Fig. 279—Spun Plate

Plate. The small plate shown in Fig. 279 will not be difficult after the experience gained in making the ash tray. Two new elements are introduced, that of turning a rolled edge on the metal to stiffen and give it finish, and forming a convex bottom (as designed in Fig. 282). Turn the chuck as before, but hollow out the base slightly to conform to the drawing (Fig. 280), then turn a follow-block with a convex curve to fit the curve of the chuck. It may be found necessary to increase the curvature of the rim of the chuck in order to cause the metal to take the proper shape. The amount of such increase can only be determined by experiment after the spinning is started on the first plate.

Start the lathe and catch the foot of the plate as before. Trim the metal, then force the rim to curve over toward the rim of the chuck. Work the metal back to increase the thickness before forcing it into the corner. Failure to build up enough metal will result in cutting the metal apart at this point.

Rolling the Edge. If a rolled edge is desired the disc should be cut with a little over a quarter of an inch added to the radius. After the metal is drawn in to the chuck it should be trimmed to a diameter which will allow the metal for the rolled edge to project over the form (Fig. 281 *a*). Prepare a wooden tool shaped like the back stick and place the point or edge against the under side of the plate at the point which is to be the center of the rolled portion. Place the back stick at the left of the metal and press on both tools. This process will bring the rim out in the positions shown in Figs. 271 *c, d, e*. Remove the tool from the under side, and with the flat tool held against the tool rest,

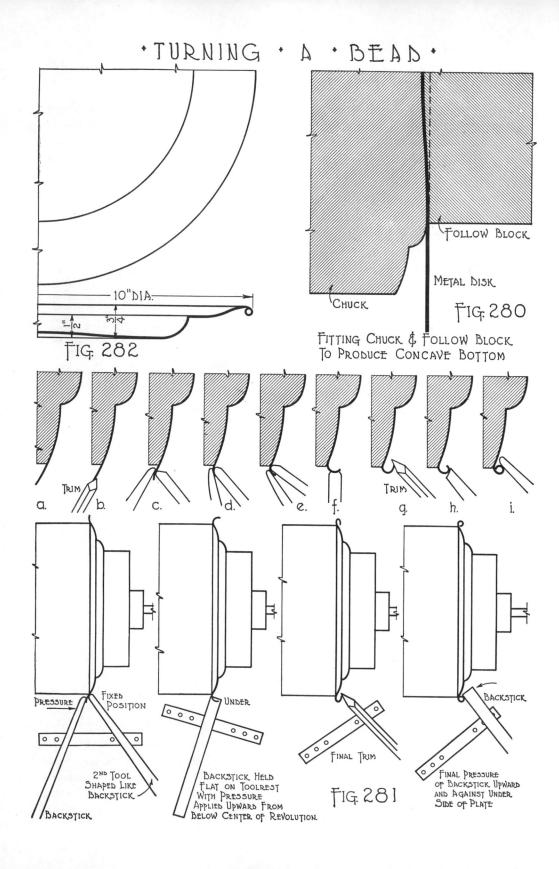

· TURNING · A · BEAD ·

FIG. 282

10" DIA.

FOLLOW BLOCK

METAL DISK

CHUCK

FIG. 280

FITTING CHUCK & FOLLOW BLOCK
TO PRODUCE CONCAVE BOTTOM

TRIM

a.　b.　c.　d.　e.　f.　g.　h.　i.

TRIM

PRESSURE　FIXED POSITION

UNDER

FINAL TRIM

BACKSTICK

2ND TOOL
SHAPED LIKE
BACKSTICK

BACKSTICK

BACKSTICK HELD
FLAT ON TOOLREST
WITH PRESSURE
APPLIED UPWARD FROM
BELOW CENTER OF REVOLUTION.

FIG. 281

FINAL PRESSURE
OF BACKSTICK UPWARD
AND AGAINST UNDER
SIDE OF PLATE

force the metal around to position (Fig. 281 *f, h, i*). Just before applying the final pressure, carefully trim the edge as true as possible and give it a slight slant inward as far as the trimming tool can be set as in Fig. 281 *g*. When the final pressure is applied it should be sufficient to force the edge into a very tight contact with the under side of the plate as indicated in Fig. 282.

Additional articles similar to the plate include: candle sconce (Fig. 283), and a butter or cheese plate (Fig. 286).

Ship's Candlestick Base. The Ship's Candlestick (Fig. 89) has a base spun from metal not lighter than 16-gauge. Turn the first chuck (Fig. 284) to shape and drill an eighth-inch hole through the center. The drill should be held in a chuck in the tail stock for this purpose. Insert a tight fitting metal pin in this hole.

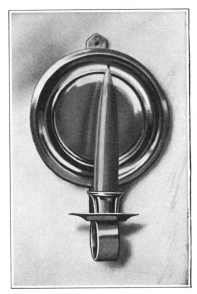

Fig. 283—Spun Candle Sconce

Cut the disc of metal and drill a hole one-eighth inch in diameter in its center. Place the disc on the chuck, bring up the follow-block to position, and draw in to shape.

Remove the chuck and mount the second one (Fig. 284), the center of which is the exact counterpart of the first. Rough out, then cover the face of the first chuck with blue chalk and hold it against the second chuck. Cut away wherever the chalk shows and repeat until a perfect fit is obtained.

Remove the pin from the first chuck and insert it in the second, put the metal in place, then fit the first chuck against it as a follow-block. Draw in the metal and trim as before.

Plate rim types are illustrated in Fig. 285, a low candlestick in Fig. 287, a vegetable dish in Fig. 288, another type of ash tray with spherical feet in Fig. 289; all of which are intriguing suggestions to the amateur or commercial craftsman.

·ADDITIONAL·LOW·FORMS·FOR·SPINNING·

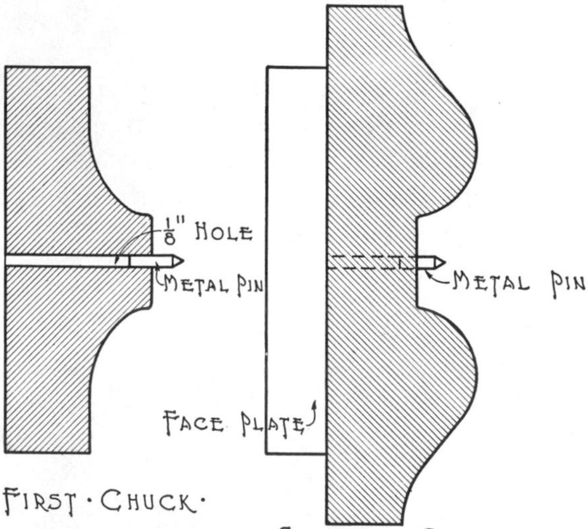

$\frac{1}{8}$" HOLE

METAL PIN

METAL PIN

FACE PLATE

·FIRST·CHUCK·

FIG. 284

·SECOND·CHUCK·

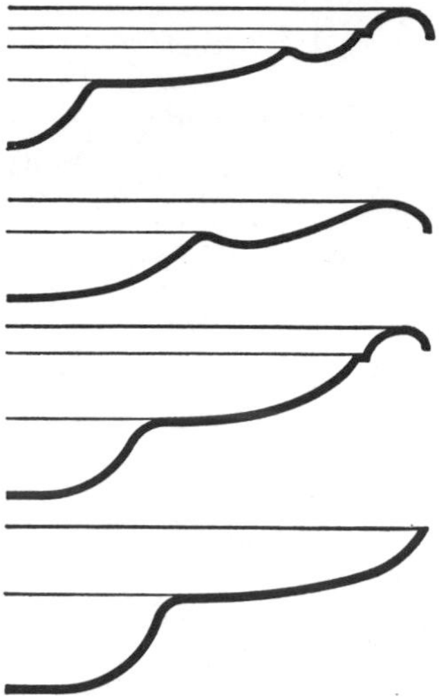

·PLATE·RIM·TYPES·

FIG. 285

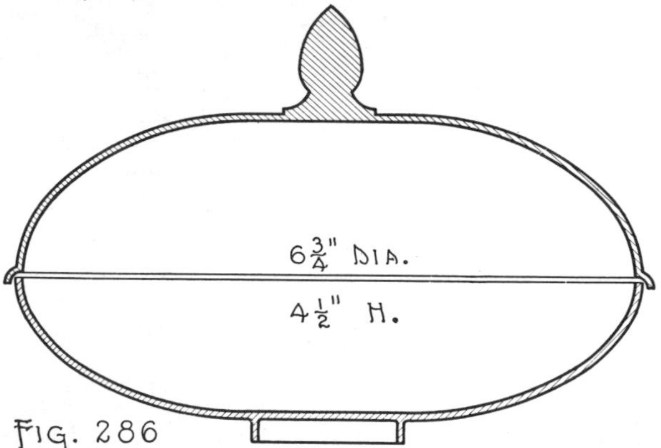

$6\frac{3}{4}$" DIA.

$4\frac{1}{2}$" H.

FIG. 286

·BUTTER·DISH·

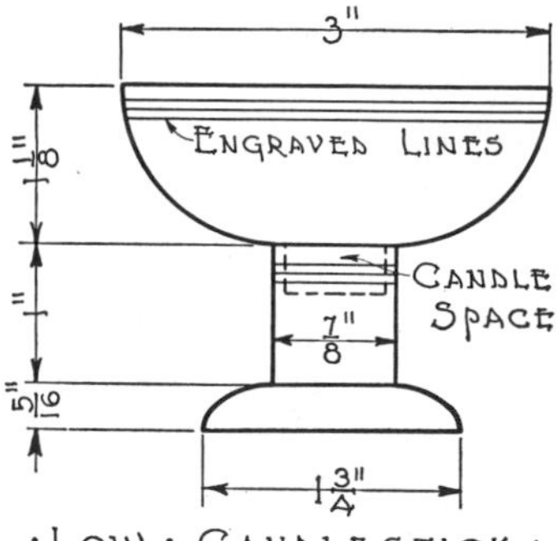

3"

ENGRAVED LINES

$\frac{1}{8}$"

CANDLE
SPACE

1"

$\frac{7}{8}$"

$\frac{5}{16}$"

$1\frac{3}{4}$"

·LOW·CANDLESTICK·

FIG. 287

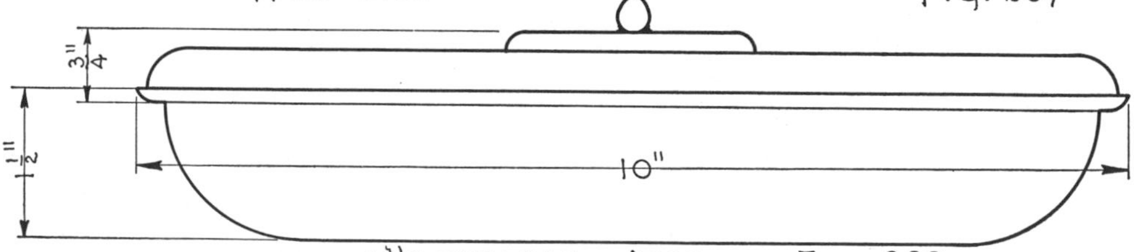

$\frac{3}{4}$"

$1\frac{1}{2}$"

10"

·VEGETABLE·DISH·   FIG. 288

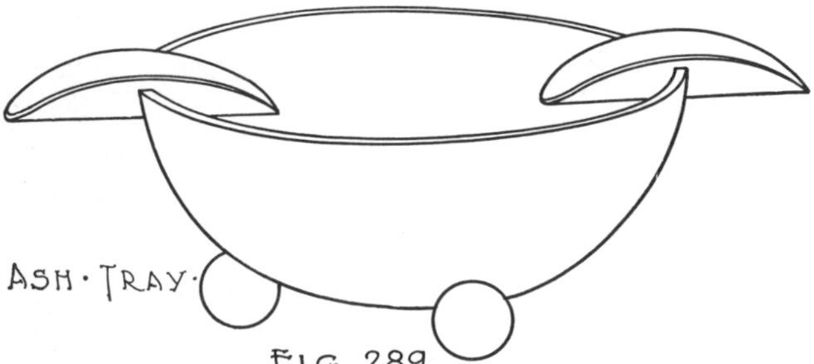

·ASH·TRAY·

FIG. 289

Chapter Twelve

Spinning High Forms

*W*HEN ARTICLES with rather tall, straight sides like the beaker shown in Fig. 290, are made, considerable skill is required to avoid spoiling the metal, and to maintain a uniform thickness.

The Breakdown Chuck. It may be noted here that when a disc of metal is clamped between the base of a chuck and the follow-block, the application of a retarding force (such as the use of a forming tool) acts in such a way that radii of the disc become levers with the fulcrum point at the place where the metal is clamped.

The application of force by the tool results in putting a strain on the metal at the base, causing it to tear apart at this point if the force is great enough, or if it continues long. This result may be avoided, generally, by means of the breakdown chuck which permits the operator continually to shift the point of strain to a new position, and at the same time shorten the leverage and so reduce the strain. The breakdown chuck has a base with the same diameter and shape as that of the final chuck, but has straight sides which make a cone with sides forming an angle of 45 degrees with the axis of revolution. The angle and shape

Fig. 290—Spun Beaker

sometimes vary for special cases. The steps in fitting the metal to this form are shown in Fig. 292. The chuck for the beaker (Fig. 291) should be made first, then the breakdown chuck (Fig. 292). This order is followed because the base of some articles is of such a shape that the breakdown chuck must exactly match the finished work.

Beaker. After the metal for the beaker (Fig. 290) is spun to the breakdown chuck, there will be little or no difficulty in getting it to fit the second chuck (Fig. 291). It may occasionally be necessary to place a back stick on the side of the metal opposite to the forming tool to offset the pressure of the tool, which tends to cause the metal to wobble and break at the base. The foot of the beaker (Fig. 293) may be cast in the same manner as described for the door knocker. Other articles similar to the beaker are the candlestick (Fig. 294), and the chocolate or coffee pot (Fig. 327).

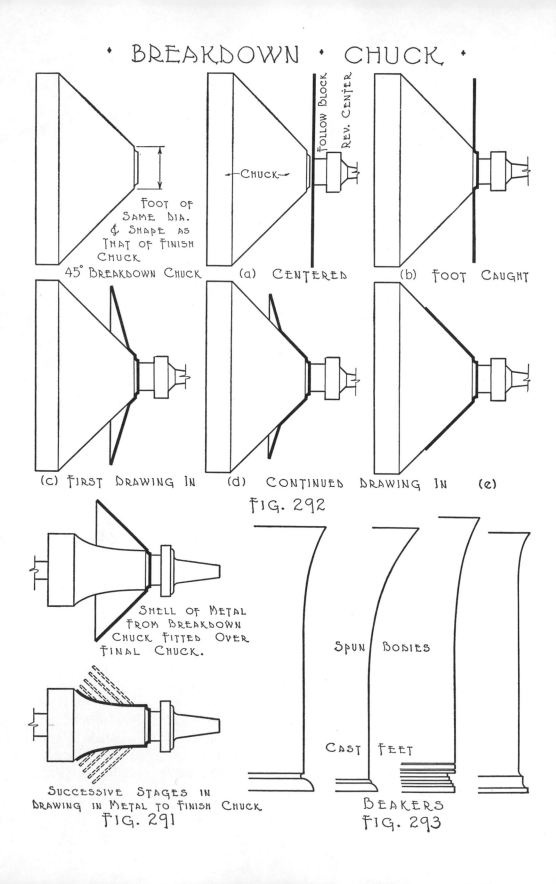

· BREAKDOWN · CHUCK ·

FOOT OF
SAME DIA.
& SHAPE AS
THAT OF FINISH
CHUCK

45° BREAKDOWN CHUCK

←CHUCK→

FOLLOW BLOCK

REV. CENTER

(a) CENTERED

(b) FOOT CAUGHT

(c) FIRST DRAWING IN

(d) CONTINUED DRAWING IN

(e)

FIG. 292

SHELL OF METAL
FROM BREAKDOWN
CHUCK FITTED OVER
FINAL CHUCK.

SUCCESSIVE STAGES IN
DRAWING IN METAL TO FINISH CHUCK
FIG. 291

SPUN BODIES

CAST FEET

BEAKERS
FIG. 293

Vase. The high vase (Fig. 295) may be spun on two chucks by making it in two parts which are soldered together. This method permits fashioning a taller piece than could be formed on one chuck.

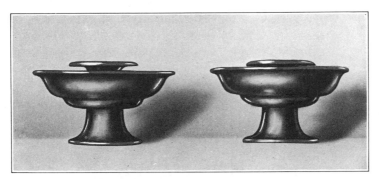

Fig. 294—Spun Candlesticks

The lower part of the vase is spun on a simple chuck similar to that used for the ash tray. One step differs in that the rim must be trimmed squarely across the metal at the point of greatest diameter (Fig. 296) and the trimming tool must not move while the operation is in progress.

The upper part of the vase is formed on a joined chuck made in two parts (Fig. 296). The steps in turning it are illustrated in Fig. 297. The foot of this chuck must be identical in size with the largest diameter of the first chuck and must continue the same smooth flow of curve.

The breakdown chuck must be shaped exactly to the curvature of the base of the final form to the point of greatest diameter from which straight sides extend at an angle of about 45°. The metal is drawn in to the breakdown chuck, then fitted over the joined chuck. The upper end of the metal should be drawn in, as soon as possible, then worked to the narrow part from each direction.

Trim the rim of the metal at right angles to the axis of revolution, then polish the surface. Cut off the base, first checking the diameter of the metal at this point to see that it is exactly that of the lower half

Fig. 295—The High Vase

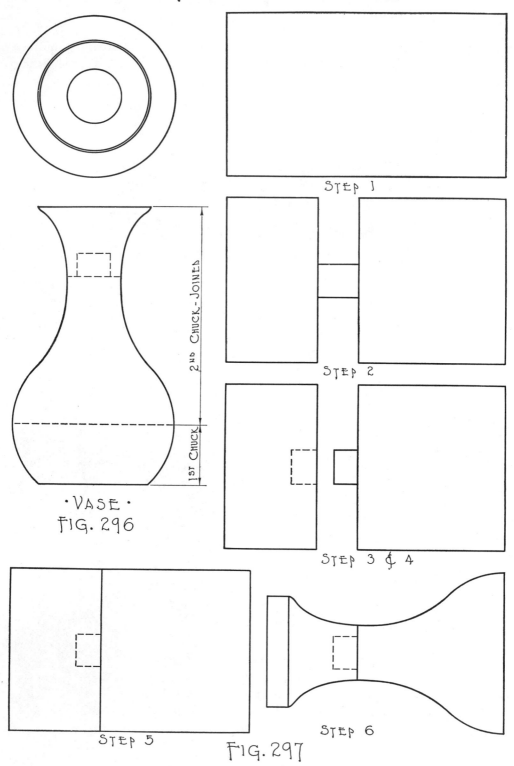

·MAKING · A · JOINED · CHUCK·

STEP 1

STEP 2

STEP 3 & 4

2ND CHUCK-JOINED

1ST CHUCK

·VASE·
FIG. 296

STEP 5

STEP 6

FIG. 297

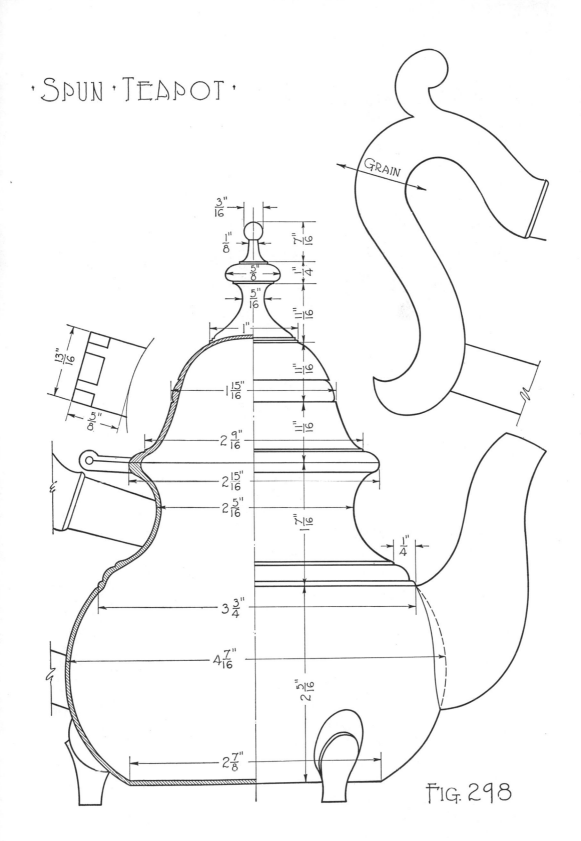

· SPUN · TEAPOT ·

GRAIN

FIG. 298

previously spun. The chuck will separate and release the shell of metal. The two parts may now be fitted together and soldered.

Fig. 299—Teapot, by Howard J. Hausman after an original by William Will, in Memorial Hall, Philadelphia

Another article spun by the same process is the teapot shown in Figs. 298 and 299.

Pitcher. The body of the spherical pitcher, Figs. 300 and 302, may be spun on one solid chuck when the chuck is made to thread directly on the lathe spindle. The chuck should be made with two hemispherical ends separated by a flat area about one-fourth of an inch wide. The bottom should be flattened to the size indicated. Spin the blank to the bottom part of the chuck in the usual manner and draw it down to the upper half (Fig. 301).

Trim the upper edge and polish. Set the trimming tool at the left side of the central flat area and cut through at right angles to the axis of revolution. If the metal slips at the last, hold it against the chuck with the back stick. Remove the chuck and take off this half of the metal, re-assemble the chuck and lower half, and trim the upper edge back to the point where the curvature begins. It may be advisable to remove the metal frequently and test its fit against the upper half.

After the two halves are soldered together the piece may be put back in the lathe on a cylindrical chuck that will fit the neck and base tightly (these two dimensions are the same). If the globe runs very accurately the engraved lines around the center may be made with the point of the trimming tool. Make a chuck, spin the metal for the neck, and cut off its bottom. Trim the upper edge slightly outside the expected final curve.

Fig. 300—Spherical Pitcher

· SPINNING · SPHERICAL · PITCHER ·

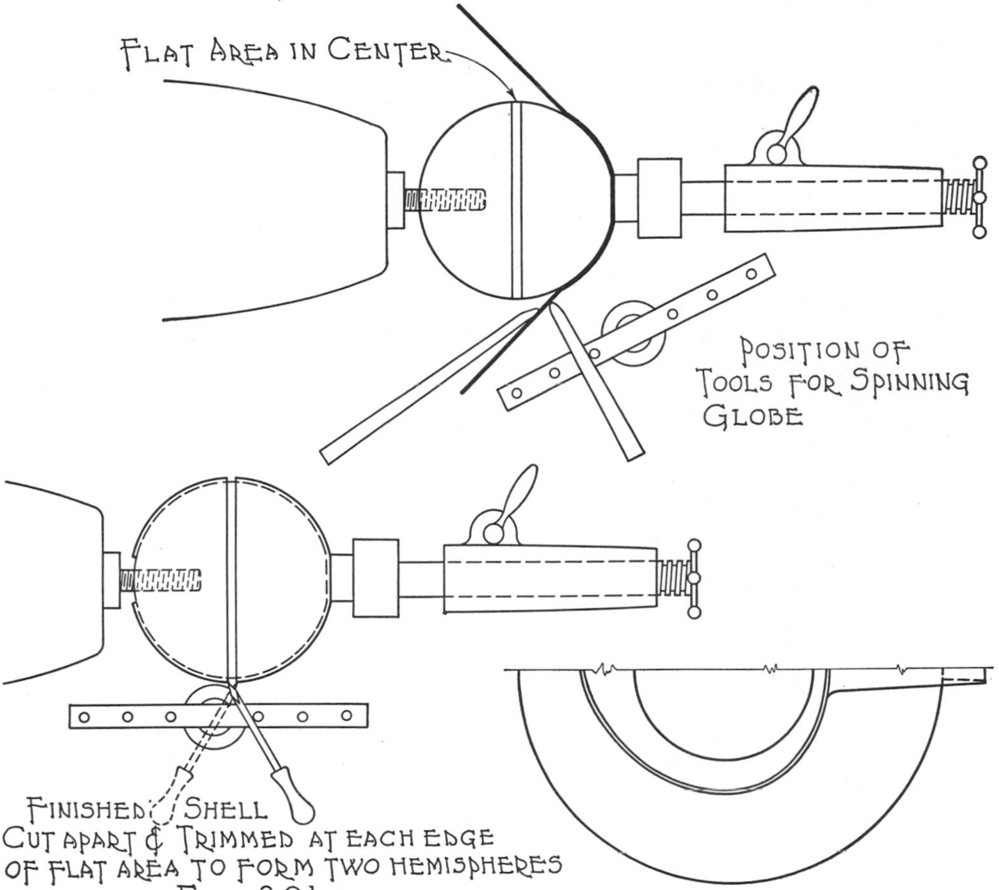

FLAT AREA IN CENTER

POSITION OF
TOOLS FOR SPINNING
GLOBE

FINISHED SHELL
CUT APART & TRIMMED AT EACH EDGE
OF FLAT AREA TO FORM TWO HEMISPHERES
FIG. 301

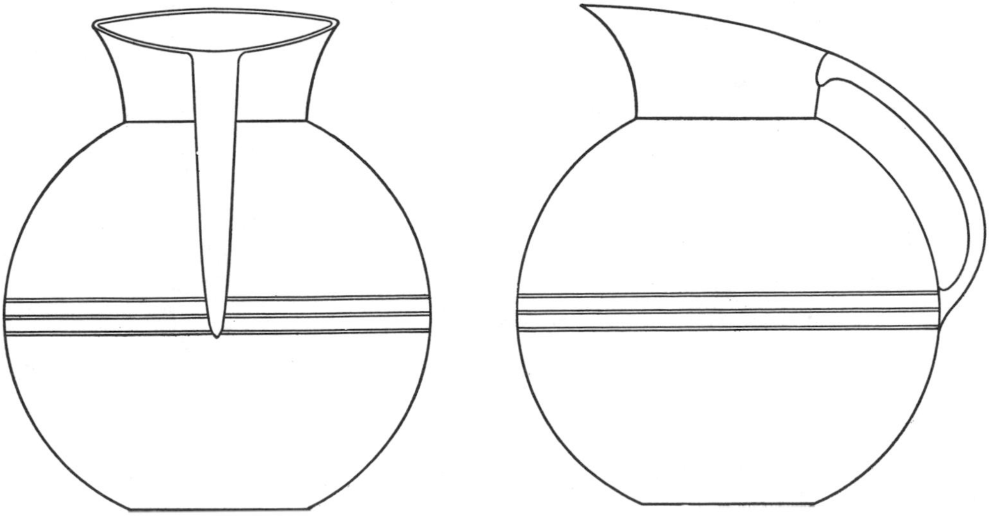

· WATER · PITCHER ·
FIG. 302

Make a pattern and cast a handle, as described for the syrup in Chapter 6. Fit and solder this handle in place, then file the neck to produce a smooth continuous curve. The spherical part of the spun pewter and copper lamp shown in Fig. 303, also offers an interesting subject.

Fig. 303—Spun Pewter and Copper Lamp

Footed Can. The neck in each of the two previous articles was smaller than some point below. The difficulty of removing the chuck was solved in one by cutting off the bottom, in the other by cutting the metal in two.

When these two devices cannot be used to advantage as in the case of the can shown in Figs. 304 and 305, pieces of this type are often spun on segmented chucks that come apart for removal from the metal.

This segmented chuck has two principal parts; a core, and the segmented shell. First turn a cylinder for the outer part (Fig. 306 *a*). Square the upper end and turn a flange on it about three-eighths of an inch high, and of a diameter sufficient to leave a wall about one-eighth to one-fourth of an inch thick after the hole is bored for the core (Fig. 306 *b*).

Bore a hole of uniform diameter through the cylinder (Fig. 306 *c*). The size of this hole must be calculated to permit the segments of the chuck to be removed through it. The dimensions of *c* (Fig. 307) must not exceed those of *b*. A safe rule to follow is that *a* should be slightly greater than one-half of *d*.

Turn a second cylinder of the same diameter as the first (Fig. 306 *f*) and turn the pin to fit tightly in the hole of the outer half (Fig. 286 *e*). Also turn a groove in the head that will fit snugly around the flange turned on the other piece.

Mark the divisions of the chuck similar to those indicated in Fig. 306 *h*. One segment, 1 in the illustration, must have parallel sides

Fig. 304—Footed Can

and be as thick as the diameter of the core. The remainder may be pie-shaped. Number the segments to facilitate assembling them. Saw these

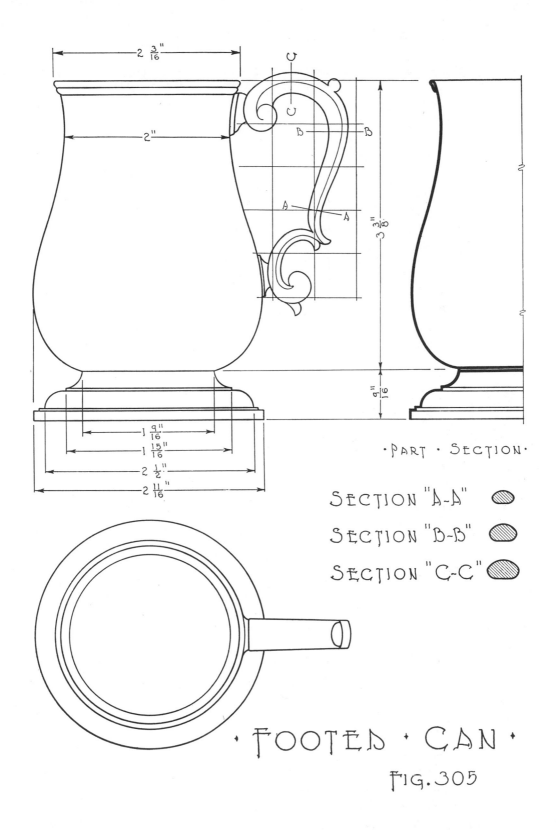

$2\frac{3}{16}''$

$2''$

$3\frac{3}{8}''$

$\frac{9}{16}''$

B

B

A

A

$1\frac{9}{16}''$

$1\frac{15}{16}''$

$2\frac{1}{2}''$

$2\frac{11}{16}''$

· PART · SECTION ·

SECTION "A-A"

SECTION "B-B"

SECTION "C-C"

· FOOTED · CAN ·

FIG. 305

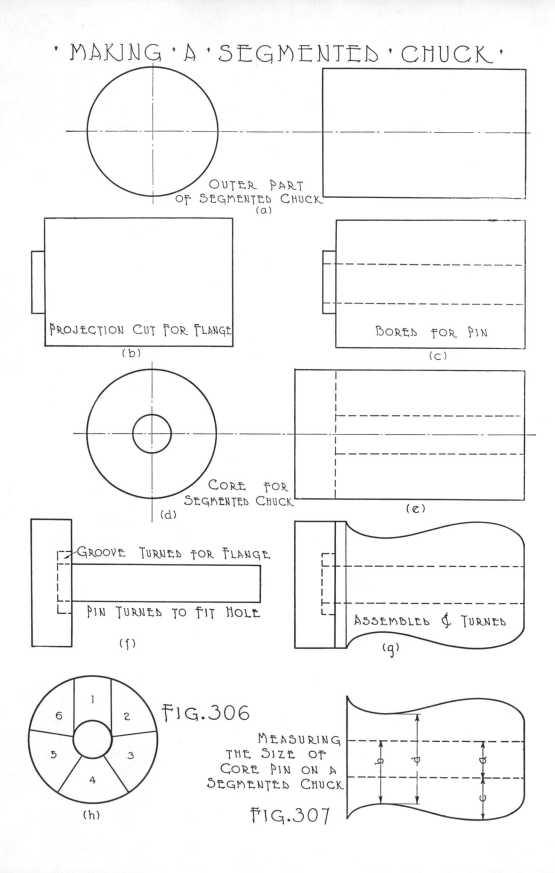

· MAKING · A · SEGMENTED · CHUCK ·

OUTER PART
OF SEGMENTED CHUCK
(a)

PROJECTION CUT FOR FLANGE
(b)

BORED FOR PIN
(c)

CORE FOR
SEGMENTED CHUCK
(d)

(e)

GROOVE TURNED FOR FLANGE

PIN TURNED TO FIT HOLE
(f)

ASSEMBLED & TURNED
(g)

FIG.306

1
2
3
4
5
6

(h)

MEASURING
THE SIZE OF
CORE PIN ON A
SEGMENTED CHUCK

a b c

FIG.307

segments apart, plane the cut surfaces, and glue hard pressboard (such as that used by the printer) or thin wood veneer on them to replace exactly the amount of wood removed by the saw.

Assemble the entire chuck and replace it on the lathe. Tape or wire should be wrapped around the loose end of the segments to hold them together while the remainder is cut to the finished size. Shift this binding and complete the shaping.

(Courtesy of Lester H. Vaughn)

Fig. 308—Segmented Chuck

In place of taping or wiring the end, better, but more difficult solutions to the problem of holding the segments together, are the cutting of a second, internal flange, Fig. 308, or fitting a cap over the end. This cap must be small enough to be removed through the neck of the shell of metal.

The metal is first drawn in to the break-down chuck, then placed on the final chuck (Fig. 310). The shell of metal holds the outer ends of the segments together, while the flange holds the other ends in place.

Remove the metal after drawing it in to the chuck. This operation will pull off the segments from the core. If the parallel piece is drawn to the center and removed, each segment can be pulled out readily.

The foot of the can is a simple spinning job. If difficulty is encountered in safely soldering the foot, a simple method may be followed. Drill four or five holes about one-eighth of an inch in diameter in the top of the foot. Turn the can upside down, apply flux to both parts, and set the foot in position (Fig. 309). Place small pieces of solder in each hole, heat the entire bottom, then direct the blow-pipe flame on the solder. If the heat is removed at the

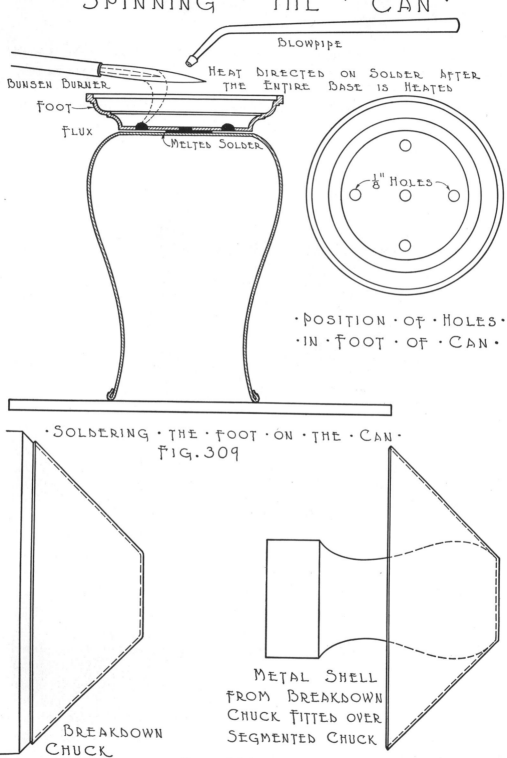

· SPINNING · THE · CAN ·

BLOWPIPE

HEAT DIRECTED ON SOLDER AFTER
THE ENTIRE BASE IS HEATED

BUNSEN BURNER

FOOT

FLUX

MELTED SOLDER

$\frac{1}{8}$" HOLES

· POSITION · OF · HOLES ·
· IN · FOOT · OF · CAN ·

· SOLDERING · THE · FOOT · ON · THE · CAN ·
FIG. 309

BREAKDOWN
CHUCK

METAL SHELL
FROM BREAKDOWN
CHUCK FITTED OVER
SEGMENTED CHUCK

FIG. 310

right time, the joint should be thoroughly soldered and the hole filled quite level with the surface. A little trimming will leave a smooth surface.

The handle should be modeled in wax as described for the syrup (chapter 4) and fitted to the can to test correct proportions. The sugar bowl and cream pitcher (Fig. 311) are spun in similar fashion.

Fig. 311—Spun Cream Pitcher and Sugar Bowl

Footed Chalice. The body of the footed chalice shown in Fig. 312 and detailed in Fig. 313, may be spun "on the air," as is the case with many articles where a neck is smaller than the lower portions. As a rule, heavier metal is necessary for this kind of spinning, since the entire strain falls on the bottom or on the small proportion that fits the chuck.

One, or sometimes two break-down chucks are necessary for this work. The final chuck (Fig. 314) has two very necessary parts: the base, which is continued up as far as possible while still permitting removal from the neck of the metal shell; and the upper end of the chuck, which is turned to the size and shape of the article at the top.

The metal shell is fitted upon the final form and drawn in at once to the neck of the chuck, using the back stick to prevent bending out of shape. Once the contact is made at the neck this fitted shell supports the metal while the tool shapes the center part. Some operations may loosen the fit at the top, necessitating occasional pressure to draw the metal in again.

Fig. 312—The Footed Chalice

FOOTED·CHALICE·&·CANDLE·SCONCE

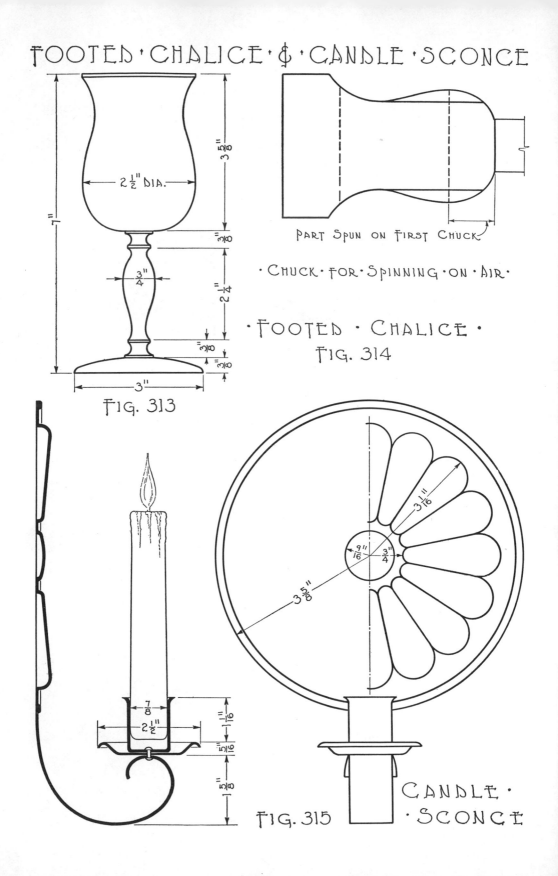

2½" DIA.

3⅝"

7"

3⅜"

3"/4

2¼"

3⁄8"
3⁄8"

3"

FIG. 313

PART SPUN ON FIRST CHUCK

·CHUCK· FOR·SPINNING ·ON·AIR·

·FOOTED · CHALICE ·
FIG. 314

7⁄8
2½"
1"/16
5"/16
5⅝"

FIG. 315

3 1⁄16"

9"/16   3"/4

3 5⁄8"

CANDLE·
·SCONCE

Fig. 316—The Caudle Cup

The process of casting and turning as described for the ship's candlestick may be used for making the shaft and foot of the chalice.

Further suggestions for the student and pewter craftsman include such articles as parts of the candle sconce. Fig 315, the caudle cup shown in Fig. 316 and detailed in Fig. 318, another form of candlestick in Fig. 317, the compote in Fig. 319, the pen and ink stand, Fig. 324, the footed plate, Fig. 320, the teapot, Fig. 321, the cup, Fig. 322, another cream pitcher, Fig. 324, the double handled porringer, Fig. 325, the cheese dish, Fig. 326, the cocoa pot, Fig. 327, and another model of teapot, Fig. 328.

Only a few of the many artistic articles which may be made in pewter and similar alloys have been mentioned. The student and craftsman will find many others which are equally attractive.

· SUGGESTIONS · FOR · SPUN · PEWTER · WARE ·

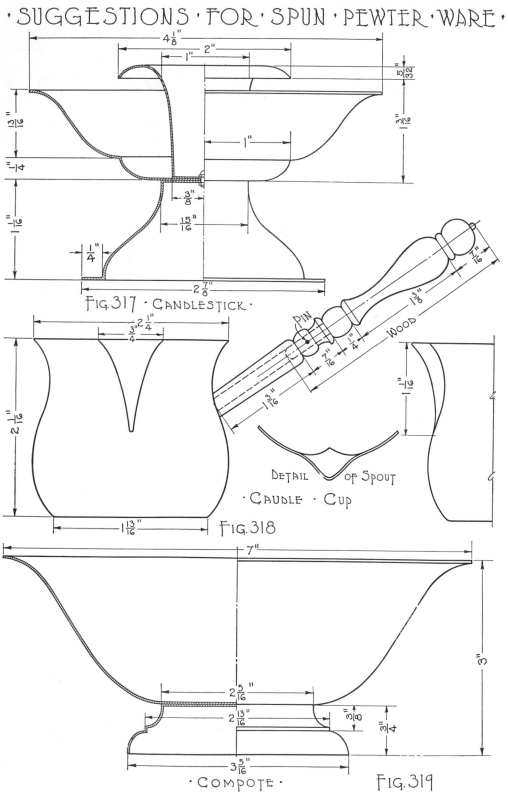

FIG. 317 · CANDLESTICK ·

DETAIL OF SPOUT

· CAUDLE · CUP

FIG. 318

· COMPOTE ·   FIG. 319

· STUDIES · IN · PEWTER ·

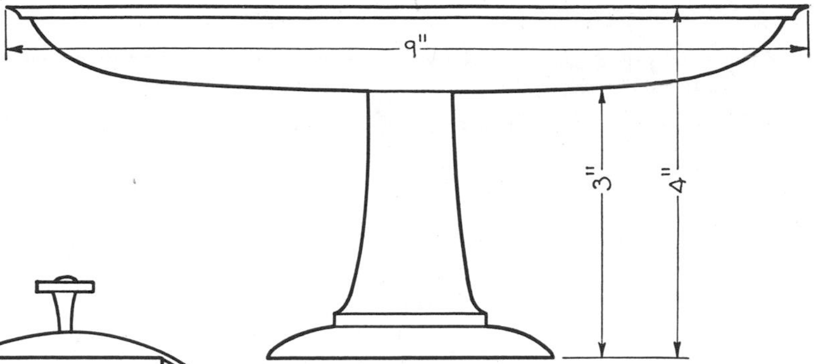

FOOTED PLATE ~ FIG. 320

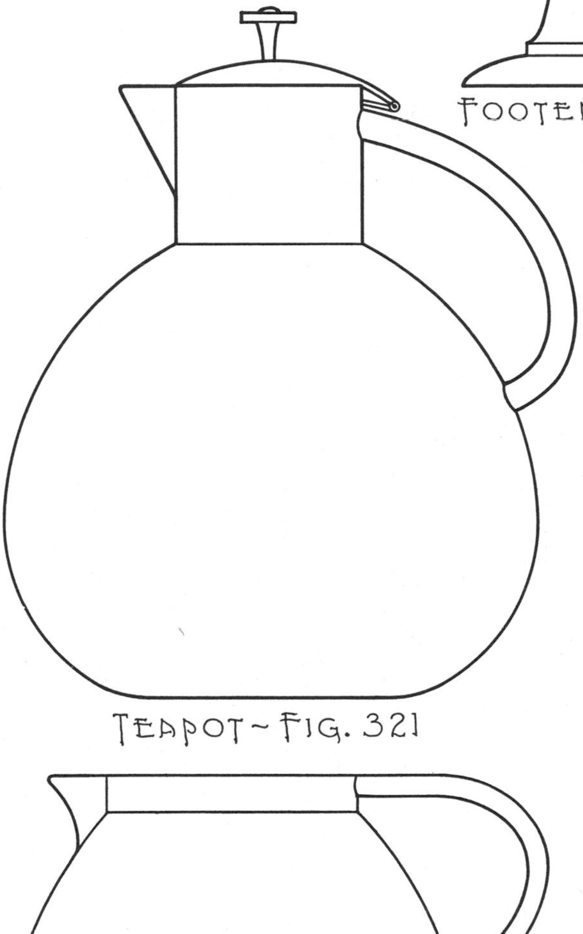

9"

3"

4"

TEAPOT ~ FIG. 321

CUP ~ FIG. 322

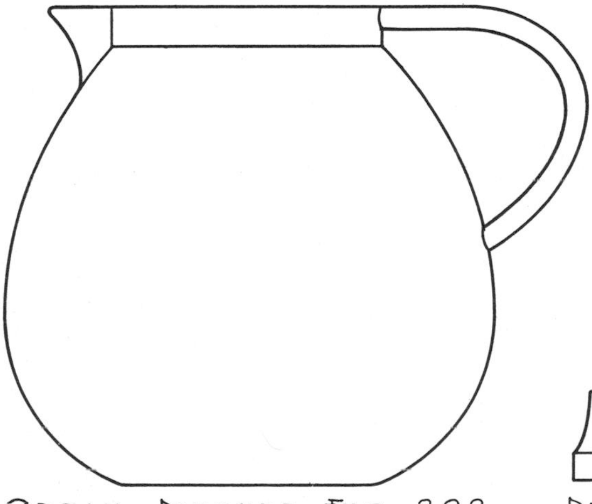

CREAM PITCHER ~ FIG. 323

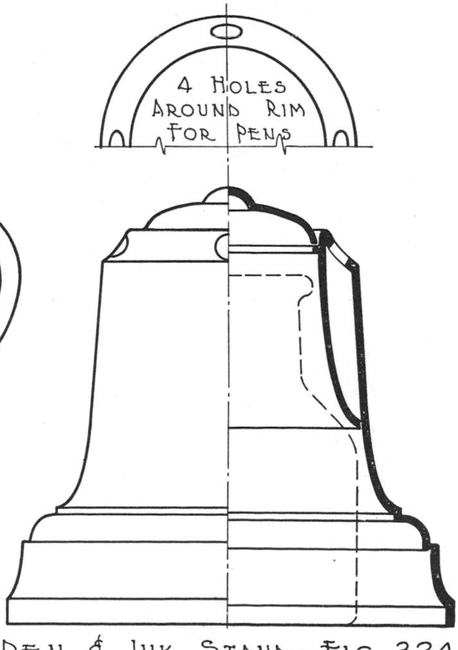

4 HOLES
AROUND RIM
FOR PENS

PEN & INK STAND ~ FIG. 324

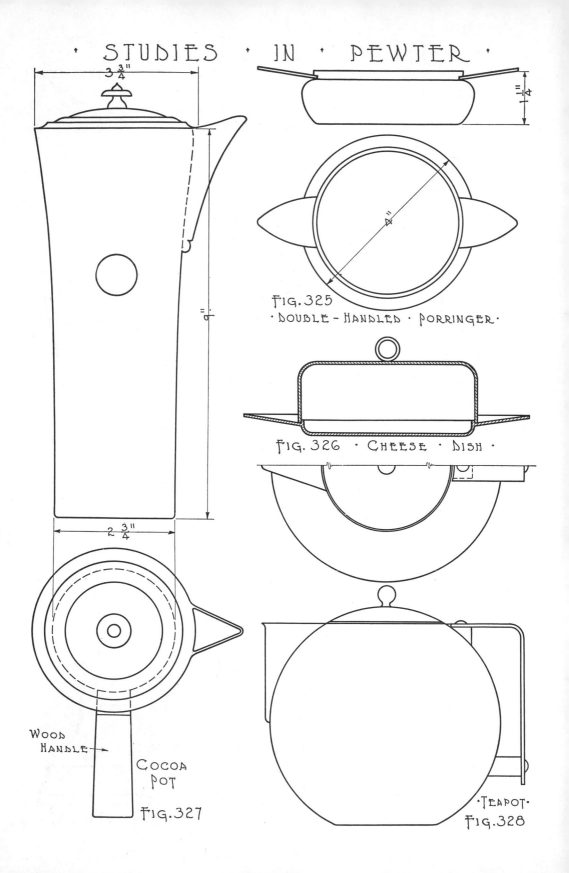

· STUDIES · IN · PEWTER ·

3 3/4"

1 1/4"

FIG. 325
· DOUBLE - HANDLED · PORRINGER ·

FIG. 326 · CHEESE · DISH ·

2 3/4"

WOOD
HANDLE →

COCOA
POT

FIG. 327

· TEAPOT ·
FIG. 328

Bibliography

Boice, W. B., and L. E. *Metal Spinning for the Home Craftsman*. Toledo, Ohio: W. B. and J. E. Boice, (n.d.).

Cotterell, Howard H. *National Types of Old Pewter*. Boston: Antiques Inc., 1925.

Cotterell, Howard H. *Old Pewter*. New York: Charles Scribner's Sons Company, 1929.

Englefield, Elsie. *A Short History of Pewter*. London: The Priory Press, 1933, 85 p.

Evans, T. Franklin. *Hammered Metalwork*. University of London Press, Ltd., 1936, xv—260 p.

Haeberle, Arminius T. *Old Pewter*. Boston: The Gorham Press, 1931.

Horth, A. C. *Beaten Metalwork*. New York: Pitman, 1930.

International Tin Research and Development Council. *Contemporary Pewter in the Netherlands*. Bulletin Number 3, London, 1936.

Kerfoot, J. B. *American Pewter*. New York: Houghton Mifflin Company, 1924.

Kronquist, E. F. *Metalcraft and Jewelry*. Peoria, Illinois: The Manual Arts Press, 1926.

Mahler, W. L. *Ornamental Casting*. New York: W. L. Mahler (n.d.).

Maryon, Herbert. *Metal Work and Enameling*. New York: Scribners, 1913.

Massé, H. J. L. J. *The Pewter Collector*. New York: Dodd, Mead, and Company, 1921.

Myers, Louis G. *Some Notes on American Pewterers*. Garden City: Country Life Press, 1926.

deNavarro, Antonio. *Causeries on English Pewter*. London: Office of Country Life. (n.d.).

Reagan, J. E., and Smith, E. E. *Metal Spinning*. Milwaukee: Bruce Publishing Company, 1936.

Reese, J. S. *Wrought Pewter Work*. Peoria, Illinois: The Manual Arts Press, 1930.

Smith,. F. R. *Pewter Work*. New York: Pitman, 1930.

Varnum, William H. *Pewter Design and Construction*. Milwaukee, Wisconsin: Bruce Publishing Company, 1926.

Museums with Extensive Pewter Collections

Art Institute of Chicago

Boston Museum of Fine Arts

Brooklyn Museums (Central Museum)

Bucks County Historical Society, Doylestown, Pennsylvania

Essex Institute, Salem, Massachusetts

Gallery of Fine Arts, Yale University, New Haven, Connecticut

Minneapolis Institute of Arts

Newark Museum, Newark, New Jersey

New Haven Colony Historical Society, New Haven, Connecticut

Old Deerfield Memorial Hall, Old Deerfield, Massachusetts

Pennsylvania Museum of Fine Arts, Philadelphia

Rhode Island School of Design, Providence

Smithsonian Institution, Washington, D. C.

Society for the Preservation of New England Antiquities. Boston et al.

Wadsworth Atheneum, Hartford, Connecticut

Many state historical collections and a large number of county and city museums should be included in the list. This is especially true of those states that have come from the original thirteen colonies and from the Northwest Territory.

Supply Sources

The following suppliers carry pewter in one form or another in quantities for craft use. Catalogs are usually available and are furnished without cost or for a nominal charge.

AMERICAN METALCRAFT, INC.
4100 Belmont Ave.
Chicago, Illinois 60641

BELL ENTERPRISES
105 Saxonwood Rd.
Fairfield, Connecticut 06430

C. R. HILL COMPANY
2734 W. Eleven Mile Rd.
Berkley, Michigan 48072

SAX ARTS & CRAFTS
316 N. Milwaukee St.
Milwaukee, Wisconsin 53202

WHITE METAL ROLLING & STAMPING CORP.
80 Moultrie St.
Brooklyn, New York 11222

Appendix D

Table of Sizes and Weights of Britannia Metal*

SHEETS

	20 ga. .031″	19 ga. .035″	18 ga. .040″	17 ga. .045″	16 ga. .050″	15 ga. .057″	14 ga. .064″
Ozs. per Sq. Ft.	19 oz.	22 oz.	25 oz.	$28\frac{1}{8}$ oz.	$31\frac{1}{4}$ oz.	$35\frac{7}{8}$ oz.	$40\frac{5}{8}$ oz.

CIRCLES

Dia.							
2″	$\frac{1}{3}$ oz.	$\frac{2}{5}$ oz.	$\frac{1}{2}$ oz.	$\frac{3}{5}$ oz.	$\frac{2}{3}$ oz.	$\frac{3}{4}$ oz.	$\frac{4}{5}$ oz.
3″	1	$1\frac{1}{10}$	$1\frac{1}{4}$	$1\frac{2}{5}$	$1\frac{1}{2}$	$1\frac{3}{4}$	2
4″	$1\frac{3}{4}$	2	$2\frac{1}{4}$	$2\frac{1}{2}$	$2\frac{7}{8}$	$3\frac{1}{5}$	$3\frac{2}{3}$
5″	$2\frac{2}{3}$	3	$3\frac{1}{2}$	4	$4\frac{1}{3}$	5	$5\frac{2}{3}$
6″	$3\frac{2}{3}$	$4\frac{1}{5}$	$4\frac{3}{4}$	$5\frac{1}{3}$	6	$6\frac{4}{5}$	$7\frac{3}{4}$
7″	$5\frac{1}{8}$	6	$6\frac{3}{4}$	$7\frac{3}{5}$	$8\frac{1}{2}$	$9\frac{2}{3}$	11
8″	$6\frac{2}{3}$	$7\frac{3}{4}$	$8\frac{3}{4}$	$9\frac{7}{8}$	11	$12\frac{1}{2}$	$14\frac{1}{4}$
9″	$8\frac{1}{2}$	10	$11\frac{1}{4}$	$12\frac{2}{3}$	14	$16\frac{1}{8}$	$18\frac{1}{4}$
10″	$10\frac{1}{4}$	$11\frac{7}{8}$	$13\frac{1}{2}$	$15\frac{1}{8}$	$16\frac{7}{8}$	$19\frac{1}{3}$	22
11″	$12\frac{1}{2}$	$14\frac{1}{2}$	$16\frac{1}{2}$	$18\frac{1}{2}$	$20\frac{2}{3}$	$23\frac{2}{3}$	$26\frac{7}{8}$
12″	15	$17\frac{1}{4}$	$19\frac{2}{3}$	22	$24\frac{1}{2}$	$28\frac{1}{8}$	$31\frac{7}{8}$
13″	$17\frac{1}{2}$	$20\frac{1}{4}$	23	$25\frac{7}{8}$	$28\frac{3}{4}$	33	$37\frac{1}{3}$
14″	$20\frac{1}{3}$	$23\frac{1}{2}$	$26\frac{3}{4}$	30	$33\frac{1}{2}$	$38\frac{1}{3}$	$43\frac{1}{2}$
15″	$23\frac{1}{3}$	27	$30\frac{3}{4}$	$34\frac{1}{2}$	$38\frac{1}{2}$	$44\frac{1}{8}$	50
16″	$26\frac{2}{3}$	$30\frac{7}{8}$	35	$39\frac{1}{3}$	$43\frac{3}{4}$	$50\frac{1}{5}$	$56\frac{7}{8}$
17″	$29\frac{7}{8}$	$34\frac{1}{2}$	$39\frac{1}{4}$	$44\frac{1}{8}$	49	$56\frac{1}{3}$	$63\frac{3}{4}$
18″	$33\frac{2}{3}$	39	$44\frac{1}{4}$	$49\frac{3}{4}$	$55\frac{1}{3}$	$63\frac{1}{2}$	72
19″	$37\frac{2}{5}$	$43\frac{1}{3}$	$49\frac{1}{4}$	$55\frac{2}{5}$	$61\frac{1}{2}$	$70\frac{2}{3}$	80
20″	$41\frac{1}{2}$	48	$54\frac{1}{2}$	$61\frac{1}{3}$	$68\frac{1}{8}$	$78\frac{1}{4}$	$88\frac{1}{2}$

* *Courtesy National Lead Company, New York City*

INDEX

Italicized figures indicate illustration numbers.
Roman figures indicate pages.